"In *The Sum of My Parts*, Olga Trujillo remi~~nds~~  h
integrity and courage really means. I~~n~~
rienced by her family, the story of he~~r~~
and an inspiration to all of us."

> —Rosalind Wiseman, author ~~of~~ ~~Queen Bees~~ *and Wannabes*
> and other books and internationally recognized expert
> on youth, social justice, and ethical leadership

"In *The Sum of My Parts*, Olga Trujillo generously gives us a rare look
into the power of community. Olga shows us how one person can
make a difference. In her compelling account of her survival she illustrates the true meaning of resilience and healing. A must-read for all."

> —Shelia Hankins, associate director of the Institute on
> Domestic Violence in the African American Community

"*The Sum of My Parts* clearly shows the resiliency of a child's mind. As
a survivor diagnosed with dissociative identity disorder, I found parts
of this book easy to relate to. Some of it surprised me, some of it made
me cry, but overall one thing stuck with me: one caring person in a
child's life can make a positive difference. I am very glad Olga had the
courage to come forward and tell her story."

> —Beth Cassell, survivor with dissociative identity disorder

"Olga's memoir portrays the complex and often misunderstood experience of dissociation with clarity, dignity, and respect. Compelling,
educational, and grounded, she conveys the immense intelligence,
courage, and willpower it takes to survive childhood rape via dissociation. For those of us on the dissociative identity disorder continuum,
this book serves as a guide for reclaiming our lives. For others, it offers
understanding of a diagnosis that is too often ignored or sensational-
ized. It is a gift of immense importance."

> —Christine Stark, author of *Nickels: A Tale of Dissociation*
> and coeditor of *Not for Sale*

"Thank you, thank you, thank you for writing this book. I don't feel alone and I can use it to help others understand what my life is like. It makes me proud to feel like I'm a part of your secret club."

—Mary, survivor with dissociative identity disorder

"In *The Sum of My Parts*, Olga Trujillo gives us a rare and courageous look inside the psyche's response to trauma. This deeply moving book carefully reveals how Olga developed, lived with and eventually healed from dissociative identity disorder, and comes to thrive. It is a truly inspiring account of one woman's quest for happiness."

—Carole Warshaw, MD, director of the National Center on Domestic Violence, Trauma, and Mental Health, and executive director of the Domestic Violence and Mental Health Policy Initiative

"*The Sum of My Parts* is a compelling book that captures the reader from start to finish. Its unflinching portrayal of the reality of sexual assault is balanced with the author's insight and hope. Readers will be taken through a journey deep into the author's thoughts and see just how she survived. Unlike any book of its kind, *The Sum of My Parts* intertwines the cultural influences in the author's life, abuse, and healing. Importantly, it also illustrates the far-reaching impact of sexual assault. It's a must-read for anyone, especially those working with assault survivors from communities of color."

—Condencia Brade, executive Director of The National Organization of Sisters of Color Ending Sexual Assault (SCESA)

the

sum

of my

parts

• • •

a survivor's
story of
dissociative
identity
disorder

OLGA R. TRUJILLO

New Harbinger Publications, Inc.

Publisher's Note

This publication is designed to provide accurate and authoritative information in regard to the subject matter covered. It is sold with the understanding that the publisher is not engaged in rendering psychological, financial, legal, or other professional services. If expert assistance or counseling is needed, the services of a competent professional should be sought.

All names have been changed except those of Olga and Casey. Some identifying details have been changed.

Distributed in Canada by Raincoast Books

Copyright © 2011 by Olga R. Trujillo
New Harbinger Publications, Inc.
5674 Shattuck Avenue
Oakland, CA 94609
www.newharbinger.com

Cover design by Amy Shoup
Text design by Michele Waters-Kermes
Acquired by Angela Autry Gorden
Edited by Jasmine Star

Library of Congress Cataloging-in-Publication Data

Trujillo, Olga R.
  The sum of my parts : a survivor's story of dissociative identity disorder / Olga R. Trujillo.
    p. cm.
  ISBN 978-1-57224-991-2 (pbk.) -- ISBN 978-1-57224-992-9 (pdf e-book)
  1. Trujillo, Olga R.--Mental health. 2. Multiple personality--Patients--United States--Biography. 3. Adult child abuse victims--Biography. I. Title.
  RC569.5.M8T78 2011
  616.85'2360092--dc23
  [B]
                                      2011023272

17   16   15
10   9   8   7   6   5   4   3

Note to the reader

Readers are advised that *The Sum of My Parts* includes graphic descriptions of sexual and physical abuse. While these descriptions comprise a small portion of the text, they are a necessary part of the narrative and important for understanding the childhood experiences that create dissociative identity disorder (DID). Readers who themselves have been victims of abuse may potentially find these passages triggering—in terms of both memories and strong emotions. If this should occur, the reader is advised to stop reading and consult a mental health professional who specializes in trauma.

For Doña Graciela, my next-door neighbor, and all those who came after her: youth directors, teachers, coaches, mentors, and parents of friends. Your seemingly small kindnesses and ordinary encouragement helped me to survive and made me who I am today.

Acknowledgments

My partner, Casey, and I have created a loving home in which I've found more happiness than I ever thought possible. In this place, I have found the peace and strength to write with perspective and humility. Without her love and support, I couldn't have written this book.

Thank you doesn't begin to express the gratitude I feel to my psychiatrist for walking the walk with me. I will always be thankful for the depth and breadth of his compassion and dedication to my healing.

Angela Autry Gorden remembered that about eight years ago I wanted to write a book. She has helped me through this process with infinite kindness and patience. I went from not knowing how to having the confidence that I could write. She is truly gifted!

Jess Beebe's keen insight and wonderful contributions to the manuscript went a long way toward making this book clear and accessible.

Prologue

Sometimes I feel like I'm in a secret club whose members understand each other in a way that no one else can. When talking with others in this club, I can say, "My mind looked like a house with many doors." They might respond that their mind was like a bus or like a series of cupboards. Saying something about having parts and having the person in front of me nod his or her head is unlike anything I can describe. In that moment, we know we are not alone.

I was diagnosed with dissociative identity disorder (DID) in 1993, when I was thirty-one years old. I have spent many years since then learning about DID: what it is, how it affects my life, how I developed separate parts of myself, and how to live with DID in a life that is full of happiness and normalcy. This book details my journey.

For ten years now, I've been a professional speaker and consultant, educating others about trauma and how to craft thoughtful community support systems for survivors of violence. All over the country, I meet people at conferences and meetings who let me know they, too, have DID. We find a quiet place and immediately start comparing notes.

Not long ago, I met a woman who was feeling devastated by her recent diagnosis. I told her, "I remember being right where you are. I was afraid of myself. Then I realized I was the same person I had always been. I just know more about myself now." She looked at me in tears and said, "I hadn't thought of it that way."

My primary hope in writing about my experience is that others who have a diagnosis of DID may feel that they are not alone and may learn more about this disorder. People need to know that the creative way they coped with trauma is not their fault. This secret club saddens me. I want to put a human face on what some think of as a mysterious and frightening psychiatric illness. There is a stigma associated with DID (including its most extreme manifestation, multiple personality disorder), and I want people to see behind the label, and in my case specifically, to see a successful, articulate woman whose DID made it possible for her to survive. There are many others like me who have succeeded despite, or even because of, their DID. We can and do lead happy, fulfilling lives, despite what was done to us. We are more than the proverbial sum of our parts.

This book is based on my experience only and is not intended to describe or define anyone else's. Each person has his or her own experience of DID. I hope that my experience helps you better understand DID, whether in yourself or others. If you've been diagnosed with DID, I hope this book helps you articulate to others where we share a common experience and where yours diverges from mine. And if you are working with someone who has DID or are in a relationship with a person with DID, realize that the person sitting in front of you is the expert, and best able to describe how he or she thinks and feels. For the most part, the stories of those with DID are likely to have some similarities to mine, but also many differences.

•   •   •

This book is based on my memories of events, some of which took place over forty years ago, when I was very young. We all know that memory isn't always perfect. In addition, most people who have studied the brain and how memory develops believe that children as young as three usually aren't able to retain much in the way of everyday memory. Yet studies have also found that trauma changes the way memory is captured in a person. Many significant events filled with violence and terror were imprinted in my mind when I was very young, and the memories I have of those events are vivid and detailed. While I may not remember the exact date if it wasn't important, or the exact year if it was a recurring event, my traumatic memories are much more reliable than my day-to-day memories. When speaking before audiences, I jokingly refer to my keen memory as a superpower. My ability to recall these events often surprises and dismays even me; I can see them and feel them as I write about them. Trauma also trained me to be hypervigilant, and I still habitually take in a great deal of information about my surroundings as a way of averting or avoiding potential danger.

You'll notice throughout the book that, in addition to capturing details of traumatic events, my mind also collected some detailed memories of events that were not traumatic. For example, I remember in detail spending the day with my next-door neighbor. She was kind and loving, and when I write about it I can feel her embrace. I held on to her and what she taught me in an almost desperate manner. Yet I remember her so vividly now because my memory of losing her is also painfully clear. Good times were usually captured to counter a traumatic event that was connected to the person or the date. In this way, I was able to focus on some good feelings when the violence I experienced got too hard.

● ● ●

Understanding dissociative identity disorder starts with an understanding of dissociation, a mental state that is familiar to all of us. Dissociation is a natural mental process that results in a disconnection of certain aspects of a person's thoughts, and it occurs along a continuum of experiences and symptoms. Most of us experience mild dissociation in our everyday life through daydreaming, getting lost in a movie or a book and losing track of time, or driving home on autopilot. These examples of dissociation all include a mild form of amnesia. Some people experience a greater but still moderate degree of symptoms without necessarily having a dissociative illness. However, some people have more severe symptoms, including separate personality states or identities within their mind. This occurs mainly in people who have experienced overwhelmingly traumatic situations from which there was no physical escape, resorting to "going away" in their head. Their minds instinctively separated out certain emotions, physical feelings, responses, or actions—and even their sense of identity.

Children most commonly use dissociation as an extremely effective defense against acute physical and emotional pain, or against anxious anticipation of that pain. Dissociative disorders are often referred to as a highly creative survival technique. This strategy is effective because while a person is dissociating, some information—particularly regarding the circumstances associated with a traumatic event—is not associated with other information related to daily activities, like going to school, making friends, or playing sports. The traumatic information is held in a peripheral consciousness, kept at a distance from the person's immediate awareness for the time being, ideally until the person has the strength or perspective to confront the experience.

If the abuse continues over time, as it did in my case, dissociation can become habitual, reinforced, and conditioned. This effective strategy can become a way of life, an automatic response to being triggered by certain situations. In other words, the person automatically dissociates when a particular environmental cue or event is similar to a previous traumatic event. The person feels threatened or anxious even if the situation or context doesn't seem threatening to anyone else. For example, in my case, if someone stood too close to me, it felt like a match for attacks that began with someone being closer than they should have been. This match was a trigger for me and I perceived it as a threat, leading my mind to instinctively dissociate.

What we now recognize as DID was once thought of, and is still popularly described as, multiple personality disorder (MPD). However, MPD is really one end of the spectrum of DID. According to the fourth edition of the *Diagnostic and Statistical Manual of Mental Disorders*, or *DSM-IV*, an official diagnosis of DID requires the following:

- The presence of two or more distinct identity or personality states (each with its own relatively enduring pattern of perceiving, relating to, and thinking about the environment and self).

- At least two of these identities or personality states recurrently take control of the person's behavior.

- Inability to recall important personal information that is too extensive to be explained by ordinary forgetfulness.

- The disturbance is not due to the direct physiological effects of a substance (e.g., blackouts or chaotic behavior during alcohol intoxication) or a general medical condition (e.g., complex partial seizures). Note: In children, the symptoms are not attributable to imaginary playmates or other fantasy play.

I developed DID from enduring a tragically violent childhood. I dissociated to protect myself from the violations and sexual attacks by my family. When an attack was too traumatic for me to experience and live with, I would cognitively leave my body and observe the incident from outside myself. From outside my body I could watch the attack on me as if it were happening to someone else, someone who looked like me. The attacker would only have seen a deeply vacant look. Afterward I put the experience into its own little room and closed and locked the door, as if splicing the scene out of a movie. At first I put whole incidents in one of these rooms in my consciousness. But as the attacks became more brutal and vicious, I couldn't afford to observe the whole of them, even from a distance. So my subconscious mind started breaking down the experiences into smaller pieces and putting these partial aspects of the experience into a series of connecting rooms: one to hold the smell, another to hold the look on my father's face, yet another to hold the deep loneliness and despair I felt afterward. Each room was to be locked shut and not opened again until I experienced a similar attack, pain, look, feeling, or place that matched what was already in a room behind a locked door.

Over time and with repeated attacks, these rooms became separately functioning parts of my mind. In other words, traumatic experiences became separate aspects of my consciousness. I like to refer to them as parts of me. For example, one three-year-old part held the first memory of being raped by my father, relieving the rest of me of any knowledge of that event for the next twenty-eight years. Instead of developing into a whole person whose memories and identity were cohesive and integrated, readily accessible to my everyday mind, I grew up as a person made up of many parts of myself—what some call "alters" and others call personality states. In the second half of this book, which details how I learned about my parts, I refer to some of them by names associated with their ages: Three, Seven, and so on.

You can probably see how this knack for dissociation could come in handy in other ways. My mind was also able to create parts, or rooms, that were perfectly suited to certain situations and access those to my benefit: a part could be an expert student, athlete, lawyer, or friend.

Some rooms only held an intense emotion, while other rooms were more fully developed, with thoughts and feelings connected to their role. Some rooms stayed closed and locked unless I needed help surviving a traumatic experience—for example, knowing how to act or what to say to survive the attack. This separateness allowed a part of me to access and draw on the earlier experience without my entire self having to remember it.

I have a form of DID that involves what's known as co-consciousness; there is always a central "me." Many of my parts had a lot of influence over how I felt, both emotionally and physically, and I didn't always have control over them or even know about them. Parts have come forward and then faded away, or have become integrated, even as a central me is always present. So in the analogy of the house, the locked doors are all directly connected to one central room. When I was younger, the locked doors opened and closed independently of the central me. I was mercifully unaware of the locked rooms until the healing I achieved in therapy made me strong enough to know about them. But once I was strong enough to know about the rooms and had access to their contents, co-consciousness gave me the opportunity to communicate inside myself, to be the authority, the negotiator, and the integrator of the parts. In my therapeutic work, this central me has torn down the walls of these rooms. Now the house is mostly just the central me: an open area with maybe a room or two still left to explore.

My aim in this book is to tell a tale of healing and resilience. However, in order for you to grasp the context in which I developed DID, and in an attempt to bring you in as a witness to the development of DID as a coping mechanism, I have described some of the trauma I survived. I believe that understanding the nature of the violence I endured is key to understanding how I survived and the importance of the ordinary kindnesses and love shown to me by people outside my family.

I've thought a lot about how much of the violence to describe and have softened those scenes as much as I felt I could. As a survivor of violence, I usually need to be careful about what I read or watch. Therefore, I have tried to keep out as much of the graphic detail as possible, to avoid triggering those of you who have had similar experiences. However, even vague references to violence can trigger sensitive individuals. Most of these scenes occur in the first six chapters; subsequent chapters focus on the process of unraveling the psychological and emotional effects of my violent past and coming to terms with having DID. You may find it easier to skim the violent scenes contained in the earlier chapters, or if this is still too overwhelming, you can skip ahead to chapter 7. You might find it helpful to ask a friend to censor out violent scenes with a marker.

Some people in my childhood figured prominently as guardians of my humanity. These ordinary and simple relationships and connections made survival possible and helped me preserve a sense of self-respect, dignity, ambition, compassion, and humor for later, when I was ready. It is my hope that this book helps those who know and love people with DID: family members, lovers, coworkers, and friends. It is also my hope that those charged with intervening in families in which there is violence will take away a more nuanced approach to their important work, informed by a deeper understanding of trauma. Most of all, I hope that those of you who have DID know that the disorder itself is an incredible survival technique. You should feel proud to have survived. Trauma has had a major impact on my life, as it has on yours, but I've learned that my life extends beyond the pain and darkness. Survivors of trauma are full of life, creativity, courage, and love. We are more than the sum of our parts.

Surviving Oblivion

1

My mom hung up the phone on the wall in the kitchen and started walking up to my room. It was a warm, humid evening and there was no air-conditioning in our house, which was actually half of a duplex. She left the fan cooling her in the kitchen and heard the fan cooling my father in the living room as she walked down the long hallway.

In the hall she instinctively stopped at a table holding a statue of Mary, across from which hung a wooden cross. She distractedly mumbled a little prayer as she made the sign of the cross: "Dios me bendiga." *God bless me.* I never knew what she was praying for, but there was so much to ask for.

In the small foyer, a coffee table displayed old issues of *National Geographic.* My mom thought the pictures were so beautiful that she never threw them away, so the piles got bigger and bigger. She wanted to travel the world and often looked at the pictures wistfully. My parents moved to the United States the year before I was born, and my mom would spend the rest of her life in the city where they settled. She continued, climbing the long steep staircase. At the top, she passed another small table, this one holding ceramic statues of Saint Joseph and the Virgin Mary. She paused briefly to mumble that same prayer, made the sign of the cross, and walked past the bathroom and into my brothers' room. My brothers, Mike and Alex, who were five and six years old, respectively, were playing with toys on their beds. I adored Mike but was afraid of Alex and stayed away from him when I could. This was the summer of my fourth birthday.

Walking through my brothers' room, my mom pulled aside the curtain that served as my door. She sat down next to me on my small bed. My room barely contained its belongings: a twin bed with a brown wooden headboard, a dresser, and some built-in shelves. It wasn't part of the original house, but a small add-on built by previous owners. When we moved in, my mom proudly told me that this would be my room; I wouldn't have to share with my brothers. At first I was glad to have the room to myself. But in the small addition I was at the very end of the house, far from my parents' room. I had no real door and no heat, and one wall was made of brick, with a scary window that looked into my room from the bathroom.

I could have had a different room in the house—one all the way down the hall, next to my parents' bedroom. Its door locked, and it had heat and a window to the outside. It had always been part of the house, yet it went unused. I often wondered, *Why isn't that my room?* It seems obvious to me now. If I had been in that room, I could have locked the door. My mom would have heard what my father was doing to me, or I could have screamed out the window to passersby. Instead, I slept in the back of the house, isolated and exposed in a room without a door, and with a window that allowed someone standing in the bathroom to watch me.

My mom didn't come into my room very often, but this evening she had some special news. She spoke to me in Spanish, the only language I knew at that age. "Olguita, I found a job and I won't be home to care for you during the week." A surge of fear and panic rushed through my body because I knew my father had forbidden her from working. I was afraid for her, and I was afraid for me. I asked my mom why she had to go. "Because your father doesn't speak English and there aren't jobs he can do in Spanish."

Later I heard him yelling at her. He said that since she was a woman, her role was in the house taking care of us kids, not out there speaking English and working. My mom pleaded with him. "We need the money, Alejandro. We are behind in the rent and we can't afford groceries. You want our children to go to Catholic school, and that costs a lot." He stormed out of the room, and the next week she started her job.

Back then, in the 1960s, if you didn't speak English and refused to consider jobs in the service industry, like a janitor or dishwasher, you didn't find work. So my father rarely worked. He told people he had a Ph.D. He really didn't, but I didn't know that then. He introduced himself to people with the title "Doctor," and when people asked if he was a medical doctor, he'd say he was a doctor of international relations.

My father was a habitual liar, even about unimportant things: who he talked to, what he did that day, and even what we ate for lunch. I saw him twist facts easily, often in ways that confused me. We always celebrated his birthday on March 28, and it wasn't until his death that I learned he was actually born on June 12. At various times he disappeared for weeks or months at a time, saying he was going to work somewhere overseas, but then he came home with no money.

My father, or Popi, as my brothers and I called him, was fifty-one when I was born. I don't know much about the truth of his life before then, despite the many stories I heard. He said that he had been a journalist for an El Salvadoran newspaper and met my mom when he was on assignment in the Dominican Republic. He was on assignment in Argentina when Alex was born and was working in Puerto Rico when Mike was born. He later covered the Castro revolution in Cuba, and he told me the only reason he came to the United States was that when Castro took over they had to leave in a hurry, which was also why we didn't have many belongings—they were given only forty-eight hours to leave the country. He said that he had worked as an aide in the Kennedy and Roosevelt administrations as an expert on Latin America. For years I told people my father was a journalist. I never discovered any evidence of his being a journalist or working as a political aide, but at the time I believed my father was very important.

My father was mostly bald, with short gray hair on the sides of his head and a few hairs on the very top of his head that he brushed back. He had a little gray mustache that he was always clipping and trimming. He had age spots on his hands and arms and wrinkles on his face, but his hands were always washed and his nails trimmed impeccably. They looked perfect at the end of his short, strong fingers. I learned to watch my father's every expression, check how his small mouth and mustache set on his face, listen for changes in his voice and speech, and, in this way, try to spot danger signals.

It was odd to see my mother and father together. Mame, as I adoringly called my mom, or Blanca, as my father called her, was tall and young and beautiful. In contrast, Popi was short and seemed old—too old for her, really. After all, he was twenty-four years her senior. I later learned from my mother that they met and married in the Dominican Republic, where her family was from. But when she became pregnant with Alex, my father left her and went to Argentina. He didn't tell her anything; he just left. My mom tracked him down in Argentina so they could live together as a family. My brother Alex was born early, not long after my mother fell down the stairs of their home. In her story of Alex's birth she never said my father had pushed her, but I always believed he did. I never saw my mom fall unless my father pushed or punched her.

I was very close to my mom and thought she was the smartest woman ever. She told me that she started school at the age of four, graduated from Catholic high school when she was sixteen, and then became the only person in her family to go to college. Her degree and her bilingual Spanish and English shorthand and dictation skills allowed her to find good jobs as a secretary. That day when I was nearly four years old, she explained to me with a smile, "I'll be working in a hospital downtown." Even though I was terrified, I was very proud of Mame. She was smart and she was going to take care of us.

And she did. When my mom got that job, my father decided she would give him all the money she earned so he could decide how it would be spent. I later learned that my mom cashed her checks and put some money in an account that my father didn't know about, then brought the rest of the money home.

I felt so much love for her as she sat on my bed, holding my hand and very gently telling me that she was going to be at work during the day instead of taking care of us. I searched her face, and in her big, dark brown eyes I found the look I so desperately needed to see, the look that meant she loved me.

As my mom held my little hand in her big one, I looked at her long, polished nails. She wore a shade of deep red, almost burgundy, and her hands looked soft and beautiful. She had long, thick fingers, or at least they seemed long to me at the time. She held my hands and inspected them to see if I had washed them. She smiled. "You have my hands, Olguita." *I have Mame's hands*, I thought. My heart filled with love for her. She always looked just perfect. Her black curly hair was stylishly short. She was tall and thin and wore makeup. Yet even though she was smart and beautiful, she also seemed fragile to me. I was always afraid of losing her. I was always afraid of her getting hurt. It just seemed like she could break so easily.

As she held my hand in hers, she explained, "I have talked with Doña Graciela, and she's going to take care of you during the day." My next-door neighbor, Graciela Hernández, was old, and we respected her for the wisdom that comes with age. Doña, a title we were taught to use for female elders, became her first name to me. When I went to her house, she welcomed me with both arms wide open, followed by an enormous hug in which I disappeared into her soft body. She seemed gigantic to me, and very tall. She couldn't have been either one, but I was small, even for a three-year-old, and in comparison she seemed huge. She always wore loose-fitting dresses, not anything fancy but something like a big cotton robe. She wore her long, white-gray, wiry hair pulled back into a bun and, like my father, had age spots on her hands and wrinkles all over. Her skin felt roughened by the sun, and to me she smelled like a woman who had spent most of her life working in the fields of El Salvador. She was a simple woman who didn't wear perfumes and rarely indulged in anything special for herself.

If I couldn't be with my mom, Doña Graciela was the next best thing. I was so excited to see her face every morning, get her heart-felt hug, and hear her say, "Good morning, my love, Olguita"—words that began a day in which Doña Graciela allowed me into her life and let me share in her activities. We would start in the kitchen, where she fixed eggs and *pupusas*, which are like thick tortillas that she filled with cheese. Then we went to the basement to do laundry and iron clothes.

Most of Doña Graciela's family still lived in El Salvador, but she lived in the other side of our duplex with her forty-five-year-old daughter and her nineteen-year-old granddaughter. Theirs was an unusual household in our culture: three women living in a home without a man. My father seemed to track the movements of her granddaughter, Gracielita, watching her leave the house and come home and commenting on the time she left and what she was wear-ing. My father didn't like that Gracielita wore pants or that she spoke English. He didn't approve of how Doña Graciela and her daughter, Señora Graciela, were raising her. "Gracielita needs to learn respect for her culture. She is a young woman who does not know how to be a woman." The way he looked at her and spoke about her scared me. He sounded disgusted, the way he would later sound with me.

My father had many rules. At three years old I knew many of them very well. Girls were to wear only dresses. When I grew up, I was to marry a Latino, have children, and take care of my husband, my children, and my home. My father even insisted that I play in dresses, which was hard because my underwear showed and kids either made fun of the holes in my underwear or teased me because I was wearing my brothers' hand-me-downs. I hated playing outside when I was wearing my brothers' underwear. Eventually I adapted by wearing my brothers' old shorts under my dresses.

During the day, Doña Graciela was alone, her daughter off to work and her granddaughter attending college nearby. She treated me as if I were her own child. Together, we listened to *novelas* on the radio, and I enjoyed her hearty laugh or her outrage at the characters' misbehaviors. I didn't follow the plots, but I laughed and acted indignant right along with her. After lunch we watched one of her favorite shows: *Dark Shadows*, a soap opera starring a vampire. We tuned in faithfully despite the fact that the show was in English. Spanish was the only language either of us knew, so there we sat, watching every day with no idea of what the characters were saying.

Invariably, Doña Graciela fell asleep in her chair watching TV. Once she was asleep, I would pull the crocheted blanket from the couch and cover her with it. Our summers were unremittingly hot and humid, and like us, Doña Graciela didn't have air-conditioning, but she never complained about the blanket or took it off. Then I lay on the couch and napped too.

● ○ ●

Each day at Doña Graciela's ended with my mom hurrying over to bring me home. After she started working, my mom changed. Even though she still had to make dinner and clean the house, she looked happier. She walked as if she were skipping and held her head high most of the time. She whistled a lot. I think her coworkers liked her and she was valued for her skills in two languages. Yet my father still scared her. Just about every day he said something mean to my mom, made fun of her in some way, or hit her. When he wasn't being mean, he seemed to not care about her at all. Her job gave her a chance to feel normal and get away from it all, like Doña Graciela's home did for me.

On a particularly bad evening at home that summer, I was in my room and heard my mom start screaming. I had heard her scream this way before and knew my father was hurting her. I always wanted to stop him and often tried to, but I was never strong enough. On this day, she was pleading with my father to get off her and I heard him hit her. Like so many times before, I ran to help her. As I ran through my brothers' room, I saw them hiding under their beds.

In my parents' bedroom, my father was on top of my mother on the bed with his pants pulled down. Her nice work blouse and her bra had been ripped off and I could see her breasts. Her skirt and slip were askew and a large hole gaped in the crotch of her pantyhose. I grabbed his arm and tried to pull him off, and yelled at him that he was hurting Mame and he should stop. He turned his attack on me.

He hit me across the face over and over and said, "I'm going to teach you what happens to girls who don't respect their fathers." I grabbed his leg and screamed, "No Popi, no!" But I knew in some distant way that I wasn't going to be able to stop him, that I had been hurt like this before, and that he was going to hurt me in a way that made me feel really bad. As he started to rip my clothes off, I panicked. I gasped for air. The room started to spin and my head felt fuzzy. When he pinned me on the floor, I felt like I was going to jump out of my skin, and I couldn't catch my breath. I thought he was going to kill me. My head felt fuzzier.

I wanted Mame to stop him. I could hear her telling him to stop, but her voice seemed flat and weak. I searched her face but found only a blank stare, and none of the concern or love I was looking for. I could tell my mom wasn't really there; she had gone away in her head. Popi deliberately hurt me in front of my mom. Raping me in front of her was a way of hurting her too. Popi told me that Mame didn't care about me, that she never really wanted me, and that she didn't really love me. And she wasn't trying to stop him. His words and my mom's seeming apathy were devastating, leaving me wondering, *Does she love me? Does she really care?*

My mind got fuzzier and fuzzier and everything in the room seemed far away. I stopped struggling and became very still. My eyes couldn't focus on my father or anything else in particular. I could no longer hear his words clearly. Deep inside myself, like a turtle in her shell, I became smaller and smaller, until finally the panic of being trapped subsided. My breathing calmed and I left my body. I felt myself rising up from the floor, where I was pinned. It was a very strange sensation to me, almost like splitting into two little girls. My hands felt weird, and I noticed that I had more fingers than I should. Each hand split and formed into two separate hands. While I could still feel the pain Popi was inflicting, it was fading and becoming more distant. At last, I split off my mind and floated up to the ceiling, where I watched in safety.

I looked down at my tiny body tangled under my father's. I could tell that it was me he was hurting, but somehow it didn't feel like me. Being able to watch the attack as if it were happening to someone else helped me feel calmer and safer. I couldn't feel or even hear anything. My father could tell from the look on my face that I wasn't really there, and this seemed to push him to make the rape as painful as he could and hit me more to make me come back. But by then I was too far away.

This protective response happened with no conscious effort on my part. My mind adapted instinctively to the terror and chaos by dissociating. Life was simply too painful to feel, and over time, I grew to welcome the comfort of numbness that dissociation brought.

Eventually both of my parents left the room. As I slowly reentered my body, bleeding on the floor, I whimpered. I didn't want my father to hear me cry, but I wanted my mom to notice and come back. Mame had seen what he did to me, so why wasn't she there to help me and tell me she loved me? I wanted to be held. I wanted to be comforted. My father had hurt me badly and I was all alone. Overwhelmed with despair, I felt hopeless. I slowly got up and, feeling no pain or fear, walked to the bathroom to get a washcloth, thinking, *I have to clean this mess up before Popi returns.* I became intently focused on using the washcloth to clean the blood and semen off the wooden floor. When I was finished, I returned to the bathroom to clean myself up, then I put the dirty sheets in the laundry. I had to make everything look like it never happened.

Cleaning up was an automatic response, almost a reflex. I've since remembered a time when I didn't clean up after one of Popi's attacks. He stormed into my room, dragged me out of bed, and whipped me with his belt for making such a mess. Cleaning and putting everything back in order also gave me a little sense of control over the chaos, which was comforting. To this day, cleaning still comforts me when I'm upset.

That summer night, I quietly walked through my brothers' room. It was past our bedtime, and they were hiding under their blankets for fear that my father would find them awake and beat them. I passed through my curtain door and glanced desperately at the framed picture of Jesus with the big heart and hands open at his sides. I looked nervously at the bathroom window to see if anyone was watching before I put on clean pajamas. I was afraid that Popi would come up behind me and hurt me again, so I crawled carefully under the bed backward. I pushed myself past my shoes and the doll heads I had put there, back behind the boxes of pictures that my mom kept under my bed, and kept pushing myself all the way back until I could feel the wall against me. I brought my knees up to my chest and quietly let out a big sigh. It would take a bit of work for Popi to reach under there and pull me out.

I felt exhausted, cold, and hopeless. My mind was racing, but I didn't try to sort out my thoughts. I just let it all flow. My racing thoughts gave way to a cottony feeling in my head, then my eyes started moving from side to side and my eyelids became so heavy that I couldn't keep them open.

I now understand that as I lay under my bed in a state of dissociative sleep, my mind instinctively worked on creating separate parts of myself. It was like my mind was a house with different rooms to hold different aspects of what I saw and experienced that night. It was a sophisticated way of keeping the knowledge of the attack away from my consciousness—the central part of me that was always there—so that the next day I could get up and function. My mind broke the trauma into parts or rooms so I wouldn't stumble across everything that happened that night all at once. One part or room held the knowledge that my father raped me. Another room held the physical pain. Others held the look on my mother's face, the look on my father's face, and the panic I felt, and yet another held the rage. And one part held the realization that Popi was the one who was hurting me and all of the things he said: "You are a bad girl. This is your fault. God is going to condemn you. You are going to hell. Everyone can see that you are very bad." I held these words and my fears of being bad, of going to hell, and of being unlovable in a part of me that would go undiscovered for years.

That night was not the first time I had been attacked in that way. At that point in my life I had already experienced so much trauma from the violence in our family that I was unable to be a whole person with a whole consciousness. Most children that age who haven't been traumatized have minds like an open floor plan, in touch with the entire inside structure at a glance. But my mind was divided up intricately. Even though there was a central room that I lived in and always had access to, there were secret doors, usually locked, leading off that central part. Those doors opened to even more doors that led to closets or a series of connecting rooms. Over time, as I was attacked again and again, the rooms developed in complexity and detail: windows appeared or dark curtains and paintings were hung. In fact, instead of just being places in which my mind stored unpleasant memories, these rooms were becoming selves in their own right, with roles, personalities, wishes, and fears. I wasn't scared of what was happening inside me, but I was terrified of what was happening in our home.

I fell asleep under my bed, up against the wall, and survived another night. By morning, my divided mind had enclosed this memory so I could be unburdened and get up, go out, and spend the day with Doña Graciela. I think my mom had a more sophisticated but similar mechanism inside of her. The day after an attack, she would also get up as if nothing happened, go to work, come home, make dinner, and get all of us ready for bed again.

Many of the rooms in my mind were dark and scary, with locked doors whose keys I could not find. But some of the rooms were bright, with lots of windows and colorful doors. These I had more control over, and I always had access to them. I captured my experiences with Doña Graciela in a bright room like this so that whenever I needed to I could revisit that part of myself and remember how good I felt with her.

● ● ●

My father was born the sixth of twelve children in a rural area of Bolivia. He was a slim man of relatively short stature, but to me he seemed huge, strong, and terrifying. In fact, he was full of contradictions. He could be kind and gentle one minute but mean and sadistic the next. He was devoutly Catholic, but he abused his family. He was dynamic and passionately articulate about politics and democracy and instilled that interest in me. In fact, I am like him in many ways. I have his bold eyes, big and very dark brown. I inherited some of his gift for oration and storytelling with humor and exaggerated animation.

But today I am everything he wasn't able to be. I am educated, successful, and happy. I have privilege and professional respect. My father had a big ego and sought respect everywhere he went, but no one ever treated him the way he thought he deserved. Because his English was so poor, few people outside our neighborhood were able to understand him. When we went out together, people often talked to me instead of him, even though I was just a kid. Eventually, my father only frequented places where people spoke Spanish: church, the convents near our home, a Latino market, and the park across from our house, where his friends gathered to talk. He only visited the homes of Latino friends and only allowed Spanish to be spoken in our house.

• • •

Popi beat my brothers, my mother, and me anytime he got agitated. He felt that his role was to control the family and teach us respect. Naturally, being only three years old, I thought this was normal. Fathers everywhere must yell at their families to control them; they must hit their children when they got out of line. But even in my youngest memories, it never seemed normal that Popi touched me in private places and hurt me by putting things inside those places. This seemed nasty and very wrong. I didn't know why he did it, and I didn't even have the words to describe it.

Since our home shared a wall with Doña Graciela's, she must have been able to hear much of what happened in our side of the duplex. She would have heard my father's yells, our screams, more yelling, then silence or crying. When I was in her home, I could hear my father yelling at my brothers. Even though I couldn't make out what he was saying, I knew it was bad. I imagine that Doña Graciela felt helpless and feared for us when she overheard the terror in our home. Several times she talked to me about bruises on my face and arms. Speechless, I stared at the floor. She embraced me and said that she knew what my father was doing to me. She told me that God would hate it and that it wasn't my fault. "God loves you, Olguita." Since Doña Graciela was older than Popi, I believed that she knew better than he did about how God felt, and that was comforting.

One day Doña Graciela came up with a plan. When I went home that evening, I was to look around our house for places to hide when I was scared. She explained that she wanted to know where to find me if she needed to. She asked me to tell her about the places I had found when I came back the next day. When I did, we went over my ideas together and determined which were safe and which were not: for example, I shouldn't go into our garage at night, but she thought the tiny closet in our basement with a half-size door would be hard for my father to get into, so I should go there if I could. She gave me a rosary and taught me how to use it. She said that whenever I got scared, I should take the rosary to one of my hiding places and pray.

This was a great plan for several reasons. First, hiding sometimes kept me out of harm's way. When my father hit or yelled at my mom, I often tried to stop him and then he would hurt me in front of her. And if she then tried to stop him, he made the attack on me more painful. By focusing on hiding, I was less likely to intervene. Second, my coming home from Doña Graciela's house with a rosary pleased Popi, who often led us in prayer to the statues of saints scattered around the house. Third, the rosary beads eased my anxiety. When the sound of Popi's attacks made me fear that he was killing my mother, instead of rushing to stop him I rubbed the beads of the rosary and prayed to Mary: "Dios te salve, María, llena eres de gracia, el Señor es contigo. Bendita tú eres entre todas las mujeres, y bendito es el fruto de tu vientre, Jesús. Amén." I said the prayer over and over, and even though I didn't understand its meaning, it calmed me. The louder the screaming, pleading, and moaning from the other room, the faster I prayed. Some forty years later I still pray, "Hail Mary, full of grace, the Lord is with thee..." when I get scared—and now I truly understand the meaning of the words.

I took Doña Graciela with me when I returned home each night in other ways as well. I whispered her words, "God loves you, Olguita," into my hand, then closed my fist as if to trap her calm, steady voice and hold her words with me. I often walked with my hands closed in fists. At night I could put my fist up to my ear, slightly open it, and imagine Doña Graciela's voice saying to me, "It's not your fault."

Whatever Doña Graciela told me, I believed. I needed to. I needed to believe I wasn't so alone, vulnerable, or unsafe. I needed to know I was loved and worthy of love. I had been taught that our elders were wise, and here was an elder telling me it wasn't my fault. I tried to make her voice in my head louder than the voice of my father when he raped me and yelled, "You are making me do this! You are evil! You are going to go to hell." I was so worried that he was right. But Doña Graciela was older and wiser than my father, so when she said that God loved me and hated that my father was hurting me, I held on to this truth with all my might.

Things went on this way for over a year. One day during the summer I turned five, Doña Graciela came to my house to talk to my father. From my position at the top of the stairs, I heard her tell my father that she knew he was hurting my brothers and me. "I can hear you through the walls," she scolded. "You know better. Your role as the man of the house is to protect and provide for your family, not to beat and scare them." She appealed to his faith: "God will forgive you, Alejandro, if you stop and repent for your sins."

I saw my father respond as if in slow motion. He raised his right arm and swung at her hard. In my panic, I felt that familiar splitting-off feeling, left my body, and floated back against the wall and up to the ceiling. He yelled, "This is not your family!" He stepped closer and threatened, "Your family is out of control. No one has any respect. If I continue to hear noises coming from your house, I will come over and quiet everyone down." He struck her again on the side of her head.

She fell back against the door and I saw that she too was afraid of him—not just for what he had done to her, but for what he could do to her granddaughter, and what he might now do to me. He called me to come downstairs, and in front of her said, "Doña Graciela just told me that she no longer wants you to visit." My head filled with the sound of rushing blood. I watched her sad, shocked expression and couldn't hear anything else he said. From the window next to the front door I watched Doña Graciela slowly walk out of my life, holding a hand to her face and clutching the rail along the porch to steady herself.

Before I knew it, my father had me by the arm and was pulling me back up the stairs. My brothers hid under their beds as he dragged me through their room into mine. "What did you tell her? What does she know?" he raged. He ripped off my clothes and hit me across the face. I could feel the rushing of blood in my head again, and then I couldn't hear him anymore. Like the turtle in her shell, I went further and further inside myself. My head became fuzzy and I went up onto the ceiling, where I watched myself stand shaking and naked in front of him. He punched me over and over, in the stomach and across my ribs. Then he threw me onto my bed and raped me. But I was numb again, and the thought that I wouldn't see Doña Graciela anymore was almost more painful than anything he could do to me.

• • •

After that, I stayed home with my father during the day. My brothers went to the park or their friends' houses to play, or their friends would come and play in our backyard. Often I asked to go with my brother Mike, but Popi said I wasn't allowed to play with boys. I didn't have any friends my age because I wasn't in school yet and only spoke Spanish. Since my father now had access to me during the day as well as at night, he began to abuse me more.

I felt lost and scared without Doña Graciela and thought about her all the time. I knew her schedule very well and imagined myself in her house, just through the wall, holding her hand as we went down the steep basement stairs. I worried that, without me, she would fall and no one would be home for hours to help her. I worried that she would burn herself while ironing. I worried that she would forget to turn off the iron and unplug it. That had been my job. She had said, "Olguita, my love, you are too small to iron, but you can help me remember to turn off the iron, okay?" I wondered, *Who listens to novelas with her? Who's making her laugh?* Popi didn't let me watch *Dark Shadows*, so I felt I wasn't keeping up with the story. *Who covers Doña Graciela when she naps?* I tried to nap at the same time I thought she would be sleeping, but Popi would come find me if I was in my bed. So I stopped napping.

I often sat by the wall at the top of the stairs, near the statues of Saint Joseph and the Virgin Mary, and prayed. I listened for Doña Graciela through the wall our houses shared. Popi caught me sitting there a few times and told me that Doña Graciela didn't want me anymore, so I should stop listening for her. So then I started spending a lot of time up against the wall under my bed, holding the rosary Doña Graciela had given me and praying.

Doña Graciela was so alone during the days with her daughter working and her granddaughter in school. I decided I wanted to see her. Even though I couldn't go to her house, I thought I might be able to run into her in some other way. So I started walking around the block to see if I might catch her on the back porch shaking out her rugs. I played ball in the backyard and kicked the ball into her yard. After hopping the fence to retrieve the ball, I walked slowly, searching her windows to see if she was looking at me. But I didn't see her. A few times I even kicked the ball so it fell down her basement stairs. Still, no Doña Graciela. I had no one.

● ● ●

My mom also looked for ways to escape the terror of our home, but other than work she didn't have many options. She didn't have friends because my father made her stay at home unless she was at work. But on the weekends, my mom escaped into the backyard to garden. She spent hours pruning her red and orange roses, smelling and admiring them one after another. She wore green cloth gloves with flowers on them and handled the roses very carefully. I would watch her gingerly pull on a thorny stem to bring one to her face, look at the flower very closely, smell deeply, and sigh. "What's wrong?" I'd ask, but she usually didn't respond. Mame often seemed not to notice that I was in the backyard with her. I wanted to know what she smelled that would make her sigh in such a sad way. *What's sad about the flowers? They are bright and beautiful.* When I reached out to the roses and grabbed their stems, I only felt the pain of the thorns so I never did smell them. I didn't like roses.

My mother had many garden tools, but I wasn't allowed to touch them, so I dug in the dirt with my hands. I loved that. The dirt was dark, rich, and cold, and every so often I would taste some of it. I liked its gritty flavor but had to do it when my mother wasn't looking or she'd scold me.

Mame took her time digging, planting new flowers, and picking dead flowers off the plants. She stared at the flowers with a blankness that made me think she wasn't really there. I often sat with her and asked her questions in an effort to connect with her. I wanted so badly to see a look in her eyes that showed me she loved me. But on many days I never found it. So instead I would play with our three dogs or look for one of the turtles that hung out in our backyard.

The turtles fascinated me. They were the size of both of my small hands held together. I squatted over them for hours and rubbed my hand softly against their shells. Their shells felt cool like dirt, and they felt rough and sleek at the same time, with wrinkles around their neck and legs, reminding me of Doña Graciela. I would lightly touch a turtle's head and watch it recoil into its shell. For what seemed like hours, I would patiently watch and wait for the turtle's head to slowly come back out. When her head peeked out, I lightly touched it again, and *poof*, she went back into her shell. I thought, *A hard shell like this could protect me too if I had one*, and wondered if I could make a shell—something I could curl up inside of for protection.

• • •

Later that summer, on one especially hot, humid day, I saw Doña Graciela outside hanging clothes to dry. I ran out the back door and greeted her enthusiastically. "¡Hola, Doña Graciela!" She responded with her calm and loving smile and came over to the fence. I climbed halfway up the fence and reached up to her as she leaned over and hugged me. She told me she loved me. My heart filled with so much love I thought I would pop. I asked if I could come visit her, and she said that my father would not permit it. Crying hopelessly, I melted into a pool of tears and fell to the ground. Doña Graciela reached down, gripped my hand tightly, and lifted me back onto my feet. She told me that she still loved me, even though my father did not want her around anymore. She kissed my hand and told me I should start going to the community center, that there were good people there and many kids to play with. Before turning away, she whispered that she was watching my father, listening to him through the wall, and keeping an eye on me. She didn't say what I longed to hear, which was that she had worked it out for me and my mom to move in with her. But I felt a little better anyway, and I started to think about going to the community center.

Doña Graciela had done everything she could to help. I'll never forget her and her seemingly ordinary acts of kindness. To this day, when I talk about Doña Graciela or write about my time with her, I still feel the power of her love in my life.

2

I quickly put on the plaid dress that Popi had laid out for me the night before and ran a brush over the top of my hair to make the tangled mess go into a ponytail. My brothers were already noisily eating breakfast downstairs in the kitchen before going to the community center, and I was nervous that I would be left behind. I ran down the stairs, sliding partway down the banister to pick up more speed, and ran through the kitchen just in time to see my brothers go out the back door. I said to Popi, "I'm going with Miguel and Alejandro to the community center." We weren't allowed to call my brother Alex in front of my father and you never knew how he'd react to hearing Mike instead of Miguel, but my brothers never let me call them by their Spanish names outside the house. It was a lot to remember.

I didn't want to be slowed down or stopped for an inspection for fear that Popi would find the shorts I had tucked into my underpants or try to brush my hair properly. Luckily he was absorbed in his newspaper and didn't stop me. I was free.

I ran out the back door and tried to catch up with my brothers. I crossed our yard, climbed the chain-link fence, ran down the alley, and entered the woods. I saw Mike and Alex ahead of me on the same shortcut through the woods and stopped to yell, "Wait for me!" Mike turned around but Alex kept going. Alex knew we weren't supposed to cut through the woods and didn't want to risk getting caught. But Mike ran back a bit and told me to hurry. I was relieved. *I'm not alone. My big brother waited for me.*

The middle of the woods seemed like a good place to change, being far enough away from both our house and the community center that no one would see me. I tugged the pair of shorts out from under my dress and pulled them on over my underwear. Then I tucked my plaid dress into the shorts so it wouldn't get dirty. With the shorts on over my dress I could sit in the dirt if I wanted to. It was a good plan, and I felt smart to have thought of it. It was the kind of thing Doña Graciela would have thought of. I reached under the collar of my dress and gently touched the rosary.

As I tucked my dress into my shorts, Mike laughed. "Stop!" I whined. He stopped laughing but continued to grin at me. Mike knew Popi's rules too. I just had to remember to change back on the way home.

Mike put his arm around me and I beamed. I focused on how it felt to have his arm around my shoulder, his hand on my neck. I felt safe because I was close to him. Mike was different when we were playing outside the house; he acted as if he was in charge. When he was protective of me with his friends or other neighborhood kids, it felt like Mike and me against the world. I had a big brother to watch over me. I closed my hand into a fist and captured the details of the feeling for later, when I might need them. Storing thoughts in my fist was a way of creating parts of myself, brighter rooms in the house that was my mind, parts that could hold on to feelings of being loved. The little part of me that was happy, loved, and safe had started forming with Doña Graciela's first hug and continued to develop with each loving touch I felt—a bright room with a colorful door that I could open when I needed to.

It was always exciting to see the big grassy field on the far side of the woods appear through an opening in the trees. *We made it! We didn't get caught!* I guess we could have walked all the way down our street, turned right at the corner, and crossed the park to get to the field and then the community center, but that felt like so much farther to go, especially because I was always so eager to play with Mike and his friends and see Mrs. Nelson, the woman who ran the community center.

We emerged from the woods into the middle of a huge park that felt like it went on forever. Walking in the direction of the community center, we passed clay tennis courts and swing sets. In the worn channels under the swings I sometimes found candy and money that fell out of older kids' pockets when they swung themselves really high. I often sat in the sand under the swings and ate the candy mixed with a little dirt. But on this particular day we walked past the slides, monkey bars, and climbing dome and across the parking lot.

The community center was a square brick building that felt like a small school. I went inside for arts and crafts, and Mike circled the building to the fields and basketball courts where the older kids played kickball, basketball, and football. Although Alex sometimes casually joined a game or two, he didn't really like sports. Instead, he liked to hang out on the grassy hill overlooking the fields, watching the other kids play and occasionally throwing rocks. Alex spent a lot of time alone, and to me, he seemed lost. He was frequently in trouble with Popi, couldn't figure out how to stay out of his way, and often got hit and told that he was stupid and lazy. "You're not my son," Popi would say. If I had been Alex, I'd have felt sad and lost all the time.

That summer before first grade, life with Mike felt like an adventure and I was obsessed with him. People who saw us together often thought we were twins. Even though he was eighteen months older, Mike wasn't much taller than I was, and it bugged him that we looked to be the same age. I, on the other hand, liked that people thought we were twins. Mike was a cute kid with dark, tightly curled hair. His eyes were big and round on a small face that was quick to smile and laugh. My mom credited Mike's good looks, with his olive complexion, dimpled chin, and perfect little nose, to my father's family. My nose was perfect too when I was five, before it was broken over and over by my father. By the time I needed glasses as a teenager, I had trouble finding frames that could fit my nose's wide bridge and felt sensitive about it.

Since I was Mike's little sister, his friends didn't want me around. But when he didn't have anyone else to play with, Mike would come get me, and early on he figured out that I played some games better than his friends did—in part because I wasn't afraid to get hurt.

Mike was really my first coach. He started teaching me basketball that spring after finding a basketball in the alley. He taught me how to rebound by shooting the ball and making me fetch it. He'd yell at me if I let the ball bounce, so I learned to catch it quickly. At first I was really bad at that rebound game, but I learned how to slow the ball in my head by staring at it really hard and seeing the seams. The first time I caught the ball before it touched the ground, Mike yelled, "Good job!" I held on to the feeling, capturing his words in my fist. In this way I created a part that could play basketball—a part that could focus on the ball to the exclusion of all other distractions. These types of "happy" and "good" parts countered desperate times and feelings and made it possible for me to succeed in school, receive praise and positive reactions from others, excel fearlessly in sports, and develop friendships.

The creation of these "happy" parts felt different from the splitting that began at my fingertips when I was under attack. Entering these "good" parts felt less noticeable. There was some dizziness and light-headedness, but it was mainly just a gentle shifting in my mind. I was unsure of where my body started and ended for just a few seconds.

Thanks to this dissociative process, I kept getting better at basketball. After I figured out how to get to the ball before it bounced, I had to learn to throw it to Mike hard and straight. "No sissy girl throws that don't reach me," he'd say. I learned how to fake out other players and bounce the ball to him instead of shooting. He taught me how to dribble with my other arm out in front to protect the ball. For a girl who wasn't supposed to play sports, I was pretty good. Mike didn't know it, and I didn't know it back then, but the part he was teaching basketball strategy to later translated those skills into thinking ahead, planning, and solving problems.

Mike and I both knew that if Popi caught me playing basketball with him, we would both get in big trouble. Despite the risk, Mike sometimes fetched me out of the community center to even out the teams. It made me feel very special to be doing arts and crafts with the little kids and have a big kid—my brother—come ask me to play. On the way, Mike sometimes put his arm around me and warned me, "Don't tell Popi or we'll both be whipped." I'd nod as fear surged through me. Then Mike would say, "Don't worry, I'll protect you." And I would nod again, my heart filling with love. I really believed he would protect me.

As the summer progressed, I developed a part that did things Mike liked to do in the way he wanted them done so that he would want to play with me. This part looked like me and acted like me, but she wasn't worried or scared.

•   •   •

One morning in early June, I woke up with my usual anxious thoughts. I worried that Mike wouldn't like me anymore, that I wasn't good enough to play with him and his friends. What I didn't know then was that anxious, obsessive worrying helped my mind keep parts of me that had been raped and abused shut away, removed from my consciousness. Although the worrying was unpleasant, it served as a superficial distraction. It helped me get out of bed, focus on something else, and go on with my day.

On this particular day, Mame saw me come out of the bathroom and surprised me by following me into my room. I had on my school uniform even though it was summertime. Popi was strict about my wearing a dress at all times, and since my other dresses were dirty, this was the outfit he had laid out for me. She knew Popi's rules, but she told me to change into a pair of shorts and a shirt with buttons down the front.

Like me, my mother had also undergone a small transformation that summer. She was doing well in her job at the hospital, and even though we were still very poor, she felt appreciated. Lately she seemed more independent, more likely to challenge my father.

I was thrilled and scared all at once. "No, Popi doesn't like it when I dress like that."

"Olguita, you can't play in your uniform. I'll tell your father. Change, dear, and fix your hair." She found my father in the living room reading the paper. "Alejandro, Olguita should not go to the park in her school uniform." I stood very quietly, listening from the top of the stairs, Doña Graciela's rosary in my hand.

"Blanca, you are going to work. You have no right to decide what happens with our children. You lost whatever right you had when you abandoned this family for your job."

My heart started pounding harder. I was afraid that Popi would hit my mom and she would get hurt because of me. I couldn't move. But my mom calmly spoke again. "We don't have the money to buy her a new uniform. Let her wear the shorts and shirts that no longer fit Miguel." There was silence, and then I heard the newspaper crumple and hit the floor. He must have thrown it. I waited, barely breathing.

My father swore. I heard him get up from the chair in the living room and I panicked. I ran into my room quietly and sat on the bed, breathing hard and trying to stop the thrashing sound of blood rushing through my head. My father came upstairs slowly, with heavy, angry steps. I froze. He brushed aside the curtain to my room and walked toward me. He stood still, examining the uniform without a word.

I held the rosary tightly. My hands started to feel that familiar splitting feeling. Then I saw that my father was holding a pair of shorts and a shirt that Mike had outgrown. He laid them next to me on the bed, gruffly told me to put them on, and left the room without another word. I changed clothes quickly, wanting to get downstairs before my mom left for work. She sent me on my way to the community center, telling me to hurry and catch up to my brothers.

I never heard my father acknowledge that my mom was right or apologize for the ways he hurt us. But he would go along with her ideas if they made sense to him, and my mom was good at connecting what she wanted for us to what he wanted. She knew what was important to my father: that he cared deeply about our culture, our religion, our language, and getting respect from others. That morning she justified my wearing shorts by pointing out that the family couldn't afford to buy me a new school uniform. He would never want the nuns at school to see me in a ripped or dirty uniform, but he didn't care as much about the opinions of people at the park and community center. So that day, a week before my sixth birthday, I stopped having to wear dresses all the time. I could openly wear my brothers' hand-me-downs to play. I felt free.

My father was unpredictable. I was terrified of him because most of the time he was cruel. Yet I could feel from time to time that Popi loved me. I could feel it in the way he held my hand when we walked to church, and I could hear it in his voice when he introduced me to friends in the community as his daughter. I learned to watch his every gesture and expression, always trying to anticipate whether his response to a confrontation, like the one with my mother that morning, would be benign or full of danger.

•   •   •

As fall drew nearer, Mike's interest turned to football. One day he told me he would teach me how to play, but for some reason we decided to play in the backyard instead of at the park. As I started to focus, the part of me that had learned to play basketball that summer came forward to learn a new sport. Mike handed me the football and told me to try to run past him to the other side of the yard. He looked mean and scary and was wearing what he later told me was his "game face." As soon as I had the ball and started to run, he tackled me. I lay on the ground, startled, with the wind knocked out of me. The unexpected tackle made me panic instinctively, but Mike also got scared by the look on my face and got off me right away.

Popi came flying out the back door and grabbed Mike by his pants. Popi yelled bad words and scolded him: "Never hit your sister! You have to take care of her. Treat her well, do you hear me?" My father lifted Mike into the air and pulled his pants down, then his underwear. A couple of Mike's friends happened to be walking down the alley on their way home from the park. They tried not to look but watched in horror and embarrassment as my father took off his belt and whipped my brother across his behind, right on the skin. I tried to run inside, but Popi yelled, "Olguita, you stay right here!"

"Popi, I don't want to," I whined in fear.

He dropped Mike and raised his hand. I watched Mike fall from where he had been dangling in the air and felt my father's thick hand strike my face with a power that knocked me to the ground. "When I tell you to do something, you have to do it. Understand me?" I lay there on the ground looking up at him. He grabbed Mike off the ground, leaned him over to expose his behind, and began to whip him with his belt once again. Neither of us made a sound.

After the second strike, the back door of Doña Graciela's house opened and out she came. She walked over to the fence and called out, "Alejandro, leave him alone!" Her back door opened again, and out walked a tall man in a uniform. It was Gracielita's boyfriend, A. J. He was a policeman. Popi had his back to A. J. and didn't see him. I heard A. J. say, "Leave him alone," in his deep voice. Popi looked at me as if to ask what was going on behind him. I whispered, "It's Doña Graciela and A. J., Gracielita's boyfriend. He's a policeman." My father dropped Mike again, put his belt back on, and slowly walked back into the house without looking at or acknowledging either Doña Graciela or A. J.

Mike scurried to pull up his pants and stood there looking very small. I ran over to Doña Graciela, hugged her through the fence, and cried into her dress. Doña Graciela stroked my hair and said, "I'm watching, Olguita." A. J. came over to the fence and asked Mike if he was okay, but Mike just kept his head down and went inside. Doña Graciela must have already told A. J. about our family, because he didn't seem surprised or outraged, just angry. I thought, *A. J. knows what Popi does to us. I wish he could take Popi away.* But he never did. I imagine now that he simply didn't know what to do besides interrupt beatings that he witnessed. The laws back then weren't very helpful.

I didn't want to leave Doña Graciela. I was afraid of going in the house. As she let me go, Doña Graciela reminded me, "I love you, Olguita. You are a beautiful and smart girl." I closed my hand into a fist and captured her words. "Do you still have the rosary?"

"I have it here." I pulled it out from under my shirt to show her.

She smiled. "Go into the house and find one of the hiding places where your father can't find you and pray, dear." I felt scared, but I went inside as she said. I walked into the kitchen. I didn't see anyone. I walked quietly by the sink, then past the stove and a small Formica table with three chairs pulled up to it. I heard my father coming down the stairs with hurried steps.

I didn't have time to get to any of my usual hiding places, so I rushed into the dining room and frantically looked around. Long beige curtains covered the two front windows. Directly in front of me sat our big wooden dining room table with six chairs, and on the wall right next to me was a wooden cabinet where my mom kept dishes and silverware.

I wanted to crawl under the table, but there was no tablecloth to keep me hidden. I ran over to the window and hid behind the curtains. They were long but didn't go to the floor, so my ankles and feet were showing. I pulled out Doña Graciela's rosary and prayed silently, "Dios te salve María, llena eres de gracia…" I heard my father stomp into the next room calling my name. My heart was pounding and my ears roared with the pulsing of blood, making it hard to hear or think. I was terrified to answer and terrified not to answer. I stayed quiet and prayed faster. My father saw my feet under the curtain—it was a very bad hiding place. He reached over, grabbed my leg, and pulled. As I fell, I hit my head on the windowsill and felt woozy.

My father dragged me by my leg out of the dining room, through the living room, and up the stairs, shouting, "Who do you think you are? I am your father. I tell you who you can talk to." I lifted my head up as high as I could to avoid the stairs, but I only managed to minimize the blows a little. By the time he dragged me to the top of the stairs, I was dizzy. Popi's yelling continued: "You talked to that old woman next door, even though I told you not to. I'm going to show you what happens to girls who don't respect their fathers." As my father dragged me through my brothers' room, I saw Mike hiding under his bed and my heart sank. Mike had said he would protect me. On the other side of the curtain, in my room, my father lifted me by my leg and dropped me onto my bed. I cried uncontrollably, pleading, "No, Popi. Please no, Popi. I won't do it again."

He grabbed me by my shirt and lifted me up. I was filled with terror and couldn't catch my breath. I heard him laugh. I gasped for air. My thoughts raced: *He is going to beat me up. He is going to do that thing he does to me. I have to leave.* Then I couldn't hear him anymore. I stopped feeling panicked and became numb. I felt my arms split off where he held my shirt. I went inside my shell and then out onto the ceiling, and from there I watched as my father hurt someone who looked just like me but wasn't me. He watched my face as he attacked me. I saw in his eyes that he was trying to bring me back, but I stayed on the ceiling, safely away from the pain and the rage. Popi eventually stopped and I fell like a rag doll, unconscious, in the corner of the bed.

When I woke up later, I was bleeding. It was dark, so I knew that Mame would have come home from work by now, but she hadn't come up to see me. I heard her talking to my brothers downstairs. My heart sank deeper and I cried quietly. I wanted her to hold me and rock me to sleep. I wanted her to clean me up. I wanted Mike to come upstairs and check in on me. I wanted him to say he was sorry he didn't protect me, that he was sorry he didn't try to stop Popi. I heard the swish of the pressure cooker and smelled the garlic and green peppers my mom was sautéing for the black beans she was cooking.

I touched the rosary lying next to me on the bed and started my prayers. "Dios te salve María, llena eres de gracia..." I got up and shuffled carefully to the bathroom. I rinsed a washcloth in warm water and cleaned myself off as gently as I could, fighting dizziness. I felt my body splitting again and again. Despair overcame me; it was so deep and so desperate that one part simply could not hold it all.

I walked back to my room, put on clean, dry pajamas, and crawled backward under my bed, past the boxes and shoes and up against the wall. That night Mame didn't even come get me for dinner. She didn't come say goodnight. She always avoided me after my father hurt me. It was a mystery to me for a long time, but I now believe my mother was pretending that nothing had happened. In order to comfort me, she would first have had to acknowledge what was happening to me. I believe that would have been too painful for her, so instead, she looked past me. Those times she couldn't ignore what happened, she blamed me. I think that was a way of minimizing how much pain I was in. And it's not such a big surprise that Mike, being only eighteen months older, was too afraid to risk coming to my rescue, especially when he had been beaten by our father just a short while before.

Back then I didn't understand that we were all coping in our own ways and that everyone was just trying to survive, and that night, I couldn't stop crying. The despair of loneliness overtook me, and I split from myself again. I felt cold and numb. A familiar feeling returned of not being able to trust anyone, a feeling that still comes up to free me from feeling hurt when I think someone has let me down. I now know that I first learned not to trust when my father started abusing me. This protective part eventually became much stronger and more complex, then each time I despaired that my mom couldn't or didn't comfort me or that Mike couldn't or didn't protect me, I would split off again and again into many parts that wouldn't trust anyone. Later, these thoughts would come forward protectively to prevent me from getting close to someone who might hurt me, to study the people I cared about for signs of betrayal, and to help me distance myself from people who were acting in ways I didn't understand. It would take a great deal of effort to get past these parts and learn to be close to others.

But at six years old, hiding under my bed alone, this early part kept me alive. I finally fell asleep. And Mike and I never talked about that day. It was as though it had never happened.

• ⚬ •

Fall eventually came, after that summer I spent without Doña Graciela. My mom was slowly disappearing from our lives. She went to work during the day, made dinner most evenings, and then spaced out either in the garden or in front of the TV or got lost in a book. My time with Mike and our connection became more important. I was allowed to go out and play when Mike was willing to keep an eye on me. Looking back on it, I find it funny; I had just turned six, and all it took for me to be out in our neighborhood playing was my almost-eight-year-old brother's promise to watch me.

Sometimes Mike did stick really close to me, and during those times I learned games like kick the can, freeze tag, and hide-and-seek. My favorite was kick the can, but they were really all variations of the same game. And since I was the youngest player and the only girl, I was often the slowest, so I got caught a lot.

It worked like this: First, we all put our fists together and one of the older kids would count off "one-potato, two-potato, three-potato, four" to eliminate kids one by one until there was just one kid left. That kid was It. Someone would kick the can as far as possible, and while the It kid went to retrieve it, everyone else hid. Then the It kid tried to find the hiding kids. Anyone the It kid saw and tagged became a "prisoner" and had to sit and wait by the can.

I was usually turned into a prisoner right away, even as I got faster. My problem was that I would get so excited about where to hide—almost panicky—that I became immobilized. Or I would scream when I saw the It kid running toward me. I couldn't help but feel that something bad was going to happen. I'd start crying because I was truly terrified, and then laugh really hard to hide the fact that I was crying, because we were just playing and this was supposed to be fun. Finally, because I got caught so many times, Mike started taking me with him to hide. The first time he did it, he grabbed my arm and pulled me, with one finger on his lips so I'd know to be quiet. My heart filled with love for him. *He's going to help me.* Then Mike told me to peek out and see where the It kid was. When I did, Mike ran and I got caught. Mike was very fast.

So there I was again, sitting by the can. While the It kid was out looking for other players, anyone could race in, kick the can, and free all the prisoners. That was super exciting. Mike always tried to free me, and then it would become a race between Mike and the It kid. I loved those afternoons and evenings playing with Mike in the neighborhood. I felt alive and had so much fun. Then, when I'd hear my mom calling us to come in, I'd be filled with fear and sadness.

Even though Mike was usually good at keeping an eye on me, when he was with kids older than he was he treated me differently. They hid from me or, as they put it, ditched me. I would run to find them, and when I'd get close they would jump out and scare me.

Then Mike would yell at me to go home. I'd feel humiliated and fight back tears as I ran back toward our house. As I got closer to home, panic would fill me. Over and over again, I'd hear Mike saying he'd protect me, and I couldn't make sense of my thoughts. They went too fast, and I didn't really want to catch them and understand them anyway. They didn't feel safe. I'd sit in the yard by one of the turtles, touching her head and watching her pop back into her shell.

●　○　●

That fall I started first grade. Mike was in second and Alex in third. I loved school. I loved the nuns and all the things we were learning. Speaking English all day was fun. But Alex never did like school very much. He seemed smart enough to me, but he didn't get good grades. Alex's real name was Alejandro, after my father, but kids at school made fun of his name. He also got beat up a lot, mostly because he was the first Latino boy to attend our school and his name was foreign to his classmates, but also because he was a loner and lacked confidence, never really fitting in. When he was in first grade, the nuns called my mom into school to explain the situation and they all agreed that my brother would be known as Alex.

This helped a lot at school and in the neighborhood, but it was awful for my brother at home. All of his papers and report cards said Alex instead of Alejandro. Most of the time my mom checked his homework and read the notes from teachers since my father didn't speak or read English. But one evening that fall, as I was watching my mom cook dinner and Mike and Alex were playing in their room, Mame and I were startled to hear my father call, "Alejandro! Come here right now!"

We all knew the tone in my father's voice: Alex was going to get a beating. My mom dropped everything and rushed into the living room. I ran down the hallway and stood by the bottom of the stairs, where I could see into the living room but still be able to run upstairs and hide if I needed to.

My father had gone through Alex's schoolbag and found his report card. It was the end of the quarter and Alex had done okay in school that term, but my father hadn't focused on his grades. He only saw the name on the report card, and now he hissed at my mom, "Your son is using another name." I saw Alex walking slowly down the stairs. He was listening to my mom trying to calm my father and hoping he wouldn't have to go all the way into the living room. I heard my mom explain that Alex had been beaten up in school and that the nuns had suggested he use the name Alex. I was sad for Alex in that moment. I could see the fear on his face. I could feel my own stomach jump and my heart beat faster. I was working hard to catch my breath. My father replied to my mom that he didn't care what the nuns said.

"His name is *Alejandro!*" he screamed. My mom fell silent. Alex reached the bottom of the stairs and slowly walked into the living room. I scurried up to the top of the stairs and sat down, blood rushing into my head and making it hard for me to hear what was going on. I pulled out Doña Graciela's rosary and started praying, "Dios te salve María, llena eres de gracia…" I had seen my father's beatings before and knew that the sounds I could hear were my father's belt buckle hitting Alex's bare bottom.

After what seemed like a long time, Alex was allowed to leave. He walked slowly upstairs, holding his pants as high as he could without touching where he'd just been whipped. He looked vacant as he passed me. As I went to the curtain at the edge of my room, I caught Mike's eyes as I walked through their bedroom. Both of us were relieved that this time it wasn't us.

Alex went into the bathroom, and a few minutes later Mame was at the door. From my room, through a space in the window curtain, I watched them. I could see Alex crying and my mom rinsing a washcloth and wiping his bottom. Then she reached for a bottle from the medicine cabinet and used cotton balls to wipe the blood from his skin. She gently told Alex that he needed to be careful where he left his books.

As I watched, I ran my fingers along the rosary and continued to pray silently. Sadness overcame me. I wanted Mame to help me like that. Tears fell down my cheeks and I felt like I had a hole in my stomach. Afraid that someone would see me, I crouched down on the floor, moved over to my bed, and crawled backward underneath it. When I felt the wall at my back, I brought my knees up to my chest and held them there. I began crying even harder, but without making a sound. I felt so alone.

"She doesn't love me, she doesn't love me," I mumbled as I cried. I wanted to fall asleep and never wake up. The more I cried, the more desperate I felt. Finally, a slow calmness came over me. My body felt the familiar feeling of splitting. I felt fuzzy inside my head, as if it were filled with cotton. My eyes went back and forth uncontrollably. Then I fell into a sleep that pulled me away from the pain.

3

The morning of my seventh birthday, I went to the community center just like I had every day since school let out a couple of weeks previously. There was a surprise birthday party for me, except I wasn't really surprised. Mrs. Nelson, who ran the community center, had asked the group of us to cut out H-A-P-P-Y B-I-R-T-H-D-A-Y O-L-G-A from construction paper and glue the letters to a poster board. My job was to cut out the letters O-L-G-A in any colors I wanted, since it was my name. As we lined up to sign my birthday poster, Mrs. Nelson came out with ten cupcakes covered in chocolate frosting, one with a candle on top. She started the whole group singing "Happy Birthday." I opened my eyes wide and said, "Really? This is for me?"

I loved it but was scared and embarrassed at the same time. I was thrilled with all the smiling faces around me, especially Mrs. Nelson's, but a fear was building that someone would take this from me. I kept looking at the faces of the children, noticing how nice they were being to me, and I thought to myself, *They like me.* I looked up at Mrs. Nelson, towering over me with a smile on her face.

She looked at me in the way that Doña Graciela had when she told me she loved me. I tried hard to let those looks and feelings fill me with happiness, but I couldn't keep hold of the happiness for long. Soon enough, the deep emptiness and sadness would creep in to take its place. As I was smiling and singing that morning, I was embarrassed to feel tears filling my eyes and spilling down my cheeks. My bright automatic smile combined with tears confused the other children: "She's crying, Mrs. Nelson." "Why is she crying?"

Embarrassed that they had noticed, I firmed up my smile and tried harder not to cry. Mrs. Nelson searched my face. She ushered everyone to their seats, then crouched down next to me and whispered, "Close your eyes and make a wish, Olga. Then you can blow out your candle." As I got ready to blow out my candle, she stopped me and reminded me to make sure I had a wish. But I couldn't think, and my tears were falling even faster now.

Mrs. Nelson told everyone to go ahead and eat their cupcakes. Then she put her arm around me and whispered in my ear, "Take a deep breath and make any wish you want." I tried, but I couldn't think of something to wish for. As the candle continued to burn, she said to me, "You can wish for anything." I was exhausted by all the emotions, the racing thoughts, and the pressure to think of a wish in front of everybody. I had never had a birthday party before, even at home.

Finally, a wish came into my head and I said softly, "I have a wish now." She squeezed me happily.

"Good! Now think of that wish in your head and blow out your candle."

I thought, *I wish I could be Mrs. Nelson's daughter,* and blew out the candle.

"Very good. Now eat your cupcake, and then we'll play some games before you go home." I took a huge bite of cupcake in relief.

Up to this point, my birthday had been so full of hurt that having it recognized in any way automatically opened a door inside my mind to a part that knew how to survive what I expected to be a painful experience. The part that surfaced at the community center that morning was vulnerable and full of the need to feel loved, and that young part captured the loving moment with Mrs. Nelson so I could revisit it when I needed to. The sadness that part showed her was the closest Mrs. Nelson ever got to seeing what was going on in our home.

That afternoon I slowly walked home. As I approached our house, I was surprised to see my parents sitting on the front porch. My mom had come home early from work, which she never did. I thought that maybe she had come home to celebrate my birthday. Maybe she would be making a special dinner and a cake for me. From a distance, my parents seemed to be enjoying an unusually cool and breezy June day. I noticed my father talking and my mom staring blankly into space in that way she did when she tended to her garden. I'm not sure what they were talking about, but it seemed serious. He was waving his finger at her in a stern manner as if she had done something wrong. When he saw me he stopped.

I felt cautious and unsure, but I couldn't contain my delight at the sight of my mom. I ran up and tried to hug her, but she held her arm out and stopped me right away. "No, Olguita, you are too sweaty." Mame was still in her nice work clothes, a sleeveless floral dress that went straight down to her thigh, just above her knee. Her hair was fixed perfectly, every curl held in place by hair spray, which I watched her put on whenever I was awake before she left for work. Her makeup was still flawless at the end of the day, her eyeliner intact under fake eyelashes and mascara, her lips a bright red, and the nail polish on her hands the exact same color.

My father reached his arms out to me. Like my mother, he was always impeccably dressed. He wore a gray suit, white starched shirt, and black tie, and his fedora was sitting beside him on a small table. When I think about it now, it seems odd to me that he was always so dressed up, since he didn't have a job. But whenever he was going to be outside where others could see him, he wanted to look professional and important. He dressed like this when we went to church or the market, and even to take a walk through the neighborhood.

"Come, Olguita, I'll give you a hug," he said, with a laugh that was big and bold, as if he were performing for an audience. His intense eyes looked through me—it was as if he thought I were someone else. I hesitated, scared. His smile was crooked under his tight little mustache. I'd seen that look many times before, and there had grown in me some understanding that it signaled cruelty and relentlessness. In those times, it felt like he not only wanted to hurt me, but also wanted to humiliate me, to destroy my spirit. A collection of parts inside my consciousness recognized his menacing look and left me with a nameless but strong feeling of dread. The day I turned seven, I didn't have access to all the memories and information that those parts held; I only knew that I should avoid my father. Fear surged through my little body.

I looked at Mame for refuge, but I could tell from the look in her eyes that she wasn't there with us on the porch anymore. She was somewhere inside, hiding from what she could not face and would not be able to stop. I slowly walked to my father and tried to give him a hug that left space between us, but he pulled me onto his lap. I felt something slowly harden in his pants. I tried to get off him, but he held me tighter. He whispered in my ear, "Don't you want your birthday present?"

When I responded, "Yes, Popi, I want my present," he lessened his grip and I fell off him. My voice was flat and resigned. I had no choice. A part of me knew he intended to give me another "present" later. This same part had come close to Mrs. Nelson earlier that day. This part recognized the look on his face and knew how to avoid a beating for being disrespectful—and knew that he would rape me anyway. My thoughts raced: *I don't want anything from you! I want you to die.* With so many thoughts running around in my head, I couldn't focus my eyes. I couldn't catch the thoughts back then, couldn't know or understand them. They were contained—but only barely—by the many parts of me whose job it was to protect me from rage that I couldn't afford to feel or express.

My mom mechanically pulled a paper bag out of her purse and handed it to my father. My father in turn handed it to me and wished me a happy birthday, then smiled his crocodile smile again. Fear rushed through me. I looked at my mom desperately and saw that she was still gone. The familiar fuzzy feeling came, and suddenly I felt like I was across the street at the small park. From that safe distance, I watched myself open the bag and pull out a Timex watch with an expandable band. I put it on my wrist as I had seen my mother and father wear their watches. I stiffly hugged my father and he pulled me in again. This time, I was further away and didn't feel fear. I thanked my mom without getting too close. She didn't respond.

I suddenly thought of Mrs. Nelson, and in that moment I came back into my body. Asking my parents if I could show her my new present, I rushed off the porch. Before I could even hear them respond, I took off in the direction of the community center, thinking, *Please be there. Please be there. Please be there...* I reached the clearing and saw her orange Volkswagen, but I was still far enough away that she might leave before I caught her. Winded and wheezing, I kept running as fast as my legs could carry me across the field, and when I reached the parking lot I was relieved to see she wasn't in her car.

I slowed to a walk, catching my breath before entering the brick building that felt so safe to me. "Mrs. Nelson, I got a watch for my birthday!" I showed her.

Her face lit up and she said, "It's beautiful. Your parents must love you very much to get you such a wonderful birthday gift."

"Yes, they do," I responded. I didn't have that faraway feeling anymore.

"Can I see your watch up close?" I had trouble figuring out how to take it off, so she helped me. I had put it on upside down apparently, because she turned the watch around and looked at its face. "Olga, do you know how to tell time?"

"Tell time?" I asked.

"Can you read your watch and know what time it is?"

I paused. "No," I said softly.

She pulled a cardboard clock out of one of her desk drawers. "This will be fun," she said excitedly. She sat with me for a while and we talked about how the big hand works, how the little hand works, and what the second hand does. She showed me how to pull out the button on the side of the watch to set the time and how to wind it. She told me to wind it every day, and to do it at the same time every day so I wouldn't forget. I picked the time in the morning when I got dressed. She thought that was a great plan.

After we were done, Mrs. Nelson wished me a happy birthday again, hugged me, and said she needed to go home. I waited while she got her purse. As we left her office, she asked me what time it was. "Fifteen minutes after five o'clock," I responded. She said that was very good and reached for my hand. I focused hard on how wonderful it felt to have her hold it. I could feel that she loved me in how much time she spent with me and the way she looked at me and hugged me. I wanted to remember all of it. With my free hand, I secretly made a fist to capture the feelings. She unlocked her car, opened the door, and put her things on the front seat. She gave me one more hug and said, "You are a very smart and special girl, Olga." I caught the words in my fist.

"Goodnight, Mrs. Nelson. Thank you for teaching me how to read my watch." As I watched her drive away, my body felt heavy. It felt like my heart was gone, like it went with her.

I turned and felt that familiar fuzzy feeling in my head as I started to walk home. I was in no hurry and took the long way around like I was supposed to, walking slowly past all the houses on our block. I saw many families on their porches. I saw kids playing in their yards with their dogs. I saw people laughing and enjoying the cool summer evening. And at the end of that street, on the corner, I saw Doña Graciela's home. I looked in her backyard, at all the windows, and on the front porch, but no one was there. I turned the corner and went up the steps to our house.

My parents were no longer sitting on the porch. I walked into the house, where my father was reading a newspaper in the living room. I smelled garlic, green pepper, and onions sautéing and heard the soft "tsch-tsch-tsch" of the pressure cooker. I walked down the hall-way to the kitchen and saw my mom making black beans and white rice for dinner. She had bought pork chops at the store on her way home and was marinating them with spices. Pork chops were a lux-ury for us, as we usually didn't have the money for such an extravagant meal. I asked her why we were having pork chops and she blankly said, "It's your birthday, Olguita."

She had changed into an old housedress and was wearing an apron. "Mame, could you give me a hug for my birthday?" As I spoke, I could see her face harden. I sounded pathetic and she was busy. She reached over and gave me a quick hug. "There's your hug. Now, Olguita, leave me alone. I'm cooking your birthday dinner. If you want another hug, your father will give you one. Or you can go out in the backyard and play with your brothers." Out the window, I could see my brothers wrestling with a football in the backyard. I didn't want to play with Alex if he was wrestling around. He was even rougher with me than he was with Mike.

I walked down the hallway quietly and turned to go upstairs, try-ing to go unnoticed by my father. But at the top of the staircase, I saw him climbing the stairs too. He was looking right at me. My heart started racing and blood pulsed through my head and ears. In slow motion, I ran into my room and crawled under my bed. Before I could get all the way to the wall, I felt someone grab my foot and pull. I grabbed some boxes to try to stay under the bed, but it didn't help. Halfway out I grabbed onto a leg of my bed, but Popi kicked me in the stomach and I let go in shock and pain. He pulled me out and dropped me on the floor, facedown. I could barely catch my breath. I panicked and went as far inside myself as I could, and then I got that familiar cottony feeling in my head.

Some of my parts knew that if I resisted, my father's sexual attacks would only last longer and be more painful. So they stepped in and kept me from fighting back. More sophisticated parts that had developed didn't have to be told what to do to minimize the pain. They were closely connected to parts that could recognize and interpret my father's facial expressions. This collection of parts took over for me.

From the ceiling, I saw my father kick me again, and one of these parts turned my body around to face him. It knew I needed to stop resisting him or I would be hurt even worse. I watched numbly as I took my clothes off and folded them neatly. I unbuckled his pants and climbed onto the bed to lie motionless.

"You're evil, Olguita. See how you make me do these things to you? I knew you liked it." From the ceiling, I listened to his words, saw what I was doing, and split off over and over. Automatically, and mercifully, my mind split the memory of this event into many connecting but separate rooms. It would have been devastating and even dangerous for me to know that I regularly accommodated his abuse. Somehow I knew that I wouldn't survive the realization that, in trying to make it easier on me, I made it easy for him.

When Popi was done, he pulled up his pants and spat on me. Then he said something he had said before: "Each year I will give you this present so that you can remember you are a whore."

I watched him leave and then saw myself slowly get up. My eyes were moving uncontrollably from side to side—something I now recognize as a sign that parts of my consciousness beneath my awareness are very active: new parts were forming, existing parts were very upset, or parts were shifting from being actively present to being shut off. Not wanting to go into the bathroom for fear that someone would see me, I mechanically used a shirt to clean myself off. I heard his words in my head and felt an enormous amount of shame, then quickly shut the words and the feelings of shame into a separate room. I put on my pajamas and tidied up, putting the things I had pulled out back under my bed and fixing the sheets. Although I had done similar things many times before, this dissociative state felt heavier somehow. Eventually I crawled backward under my bed and arranged the boxes around me.

I had barely started praying the Hail Mary before I fell asleep. As usual, I woke up during the night and climbed into bed. This time, though, I remembered that I hadn't eaten my birthday dinner and that my mom never had come up to get me. This was perhaps the deepest despair I had ever faced—a deep, dark hole that threatened to consume me. But again my mind instinctively took over and divided the despair into smaller, manageable parts. Each part held only a little bit of the feeling, and those parts were never to be allowed to connect.

The next morning I awoke full of anxiety. I thought about Mrs. Nelson and replayed all the things she had said to me the previous day, my birthday. I saw her laughing and smiling and could feel her big hand holding mine as we walked out of the community center together. I lay in bed trying to calm the anxiety, reminding myself of the ways that I could tell I was special to her: She always smiled when she saw me. She never corrected me in class. In front of everyone, she would comment about how smart and creative I was. It seemed that she especially liked me when I looked happy, so I worried about whether I looked happy. I remembered that I had cried when we celebrated my birthday, so I was afraid she wouldn't like me as much that next day. I got up, got dressed, brushed my teeth, washed my face, and came back into my room to stand in front of the mirror.

My thick, black, wavy hair was all over the place, so I brushed the top and then created my favorite hairstyle: a part down the middle and pigtails on either side of my face. The part was crooked and the pigtails were lopsided. As usual, some of the hair on the back of my head didn't end up in either pigtail. After I was done, I carefully examined the features on my face.

I looked at my dark eyes and made them big and then small, then shifted them from side to side, then scrunched them up and kept them open just barely enough to be able to see. I smiled hard and looked at the corners of my eyes to see if I had lines there like Mrs.

Nelson did. I was disappointed to discover I didn't. I loved to see Mrs. Nelson smile; it made the lines at the corners of her eyes show, and I thought that made her look really happy.

I tried not to look too long at my eyes. With my index finger, I traced the top of my nose. I touched where it had been broken but didn't dwell on how it had happened. Instead, I turned to my mouth. When I smiled even a little, my round cheeks caved into two very large dimples that I often got compliments on. I liked putting my fingers in them. So I tried different smiles that showed my dimples. First I tried smiling without opening my mouth. That was okay, but I didn't look happy enough, especially in the eyes. I opened my mouth a little—still not quite right. I smiled hard, raised my eyes, opened my mouth, and there it was: I looked happy. I walked away from the mirror then jumped back, smiling hard to see if I could do it again. I could. I pretended to laugh, and then I laughed even harder. I wanted to find just the right laugh to show people how happy I was.

I went through this routine most mornings that summer, wanting desperately to be as happy as Mrs. Nelson looked, wanting to be happy so she would keep loving me. The perfect smile and laugh I crafted that summer stayed with me for most of my life, so I could always put on an instant look of happiness.

• • •

Being at the community center was very different than being at home. There wasn't much laughter at home. My father laughed, but only in a mean way, laughing at my mom's accent when she spoke English or making fun of her cooking and cleaning. When we came home dirty or with scrapes and bruises, he blamed her. He ridiculed her for working, for not being home where she belonged, and accused her of being a bad mother, wife, and homemaker. He knew she had a deep sense of pride about being a good mother, so his words bothered her a lot. She was very serious that summer.

Since Mame had started working, she seemed stronger, and in response my father became more volatile and unpredictable. At the hospital where she worked, people liked my mom. She was smart and capable, and they appreciated it. Her English was improving, and she had more friends in the neighborhood. Some of them spoke only English, so my father couldn't communicate with them very well. Popi was of a different generation and more old-fashioned in his beliefs about culture and family. He knew more English than he let on, but he wouldn't speak it because he didn't think he was fluent enough to sound smart.

Alex, Mike, and I were speaking more English now too. Popi, increasingly enraged at this, started setting new rules. One night he decided that we were no longer allowed to speak English at home under any circumstances—even if someone who didn't speak Spanish, like friends from school, called us on the telephone. If we needed help from Mame on homework, we couldn't talk to her about it in English. When I forgot and spoke to my mom in English, which I often did, my father's response was swift and painful.

As Popi became increasingly agitated, his attacks on me became more frequent and brutal. A few weeks after my birthday, Popi woke me in the middle of the night by clasping his hand over my mouth. He pinned me down and slipped himself into my bed, pushing my little body over. Terror rushed through me and I whimpered, "No, Popi, no. Don't do this to me."

His eyes tightened angrily. He grabbed my head with both hands and slammed it against the headboard a couple of times and then hissed at me, "It's not my fault. You do this to me." I panicked and withdrew like one of the turtles in the backyard. That night I watched from the safety of the ceiling as my father raped me in a way that was even more violent than before. He didn't seem to know who I was. He seemed to lose himself in the pleasure and, in the middle, turned me around and raped me in a new place. I instinctively split off again, my ears muffled not to hear the sounds he was making. A new part came forward to hold this unexpected form of abuse and the intense pain and take it away. Another part came forward to pray, "Hail Mary, full of grace…" Suddenly I could hear Doña Graciela: "It's not your fault, Olguita." I focused on her words, her voice, her face, her hug, and how loved I felt by her.

After Popi left I cried quietly. I slowly got out of bed, ran a washcloth under warm water in the bathroom, and carefully wiped myself clean. I wanted my mom. I wanted to be held, wanted someone to comfort me. I missed Doña Graciela. In my bedroom I wiped off my bed. I thought of Mike hiding under his covers in the bedroom next door. He had said he wouldn't let anyone hurt me. I started crying again, very quietly, thinking, *How can my brothers not do anything? How can Mame still be asleep? Popi didn't even try to be quiet. I didn't make a noise, but he was loud. Everyone heard what he was doing to me.* I was overcome with the loneliness of knowing no one tried to stop him.

The next morning my mind mercifully distracted me, resuming the worries about Mrs. Nelson and whether she would still like me. As that summer went on, I obsessed about her more and more. Thankfully, she always seemed to have time for me. I spent every moment I could at the community center helping her, playing with the other kids, and taking her arts and crafts classes. I made pot holders and ashtrays and painted picture after picture. She loved them all.

As summer drew to a close, I looked forward to starting school but also felt a deep sense of dread that fall was coming. Some parts inside of me were aware that I was abused more during the fall and winter because I was more accessible to my father; the days were shorter and I had fewer places to go other than school. This apprehension about summer ending stayed with me for many years but I didn't consciously acknowledge it until much later in life.

On my first day of second grade, I met Sister Mary Joseph. She was young, probably just a few years out of college. I could see in her eyes a sense of peace, a gentle calm that I gravitated toward. Sister Mary Joseph knew me, sort of, from having my brothers in her classes for the past two years. I was surprised that she could pronounce my name with such ease. Sister Mary George, my first-grade teacher, had also taught my brothers, but she still struggled with my name and my limited English. I always felt like I bothered her—that I was someone she had to slow down for, someone with a name she couldn't pronounce.

Sister Mary Joseph paid a lot of attention to me right from the start of the school year. Maybe she knew something was going on at home and was watching over me. I'm not sure what she knew, but she did notice everything. She often pulled me aside to ask where the bruises on my hands and fingers came from. She noticed my absences from school and asked me about them in private, and she noticed the bruising around my nose when my father broke it and quietly asked about that, too. But I had been trained to be silent on the topic of what was going on at home. My father had shown me that I could lose people, no matter how much they cared about me.

Early in the school year, a police officer came to our class and told us who the police were and what they did: protect people. One night not long after that, I was in my bedroom and heard my mom screaming in the kitchen. Terrified, I ran downstairs to help her. My mother was on the floor crying, bleeding from her lip. My father must have punched her. He was standing over her with a knife in his hand, yelling something. I mustered up as much courage as I could find and found the phone in the living room. I called the police, just as they had instructed us to do. I told the woman who answered that my father was killing my mother.

My mom heard me and yelled out, "No, Olguita!" My father strode over and hung up the phone, but not before I had given the woman our address. He slapped me several times. Then he composed himself and sat in the living room to wait for the police. He told me that when they arrived, I should open the door and get rid of them. My mom cleaned herself off and waited nervously in the foyer.

When they came, I opened the door. All three of us stood together in the entryway. The police tried to talk to my father but stopped when they realized he didn't speak English. They tried to talk to my mother, but she was so upset that her Dominican accent was too strong for them to understand her. Then they asked me what happened. I looked at the floor and made up a story. I said I had learned about them in school and called just to see if they would come. They stood in our foyer for a few more minutes as if they didn't know whether to stay or go. Finally, one officer knelt down to look at my face and said sternly but gently, "Only call us when there is a real emergency." I nodded and they left.

My father told my mom and me to wait in the foyer. He disappeared into the basement and came back with one of our three little dogs. Without saying a word, Popi killed the dog right there in the foyer and left him dead beside me. My mom and I never spoke about this to each other, but I think we both understood his message: He would kill one of us if I ever called the police again.

I didn't want to lose Sister Mary Joseph like I had lost Doña Graciela or risk having someone else confront my father, so I became creative when she asked me about the bruises. My mom wrote notes excusing my absences from school and made sure to tell me what the notes said so I could say the same thing. Nevertheless, I was comforted by the thought that Sister Mary Joseph was watching over me. She made it a practice to meet with my mother regularly, as she had when she'd taught my brothers, saying she wanted to update my mother on the progress we made in school.

Sister Mary Joseph's early discussions with my mom were about my schoolwork, but they changed a month or so into the school year. Soon she was also asking my mom about my bruises, my illnesses, and how tired I seemed. From the back of the room, while I pretended to focus on my coloring book, I listened carefully to their soft conversations. I heard my mom explain all of these things as a result of my being a tomboy. Sister Mary Joseph never challenged my mother's explanations or pushed for more information, but she did suggest a variety of after-school activities: things I could do to learn more English, study Catholicism, or improve my written Spanish. Eventually, she encouraged my mom to let me join the school basketball team. Naturally, my mom agreed with each suggestion, and with each new activity I got to spend more time with Sister Mary Joseph at school or at the convent where she lived.

I wanted to be just like Sister Mary Joseph and announced to my mom that when I grew up I was going to be a nun. Not only did I think Sister Mary Joseph was kind and wise, I'd also heard that nuns don't pay taxes. I knew that taxes were bad because I could feel the tension they created in our home. I also wanted to live the way Sister Mary Joseph did, in a convent with other kind nuns. There seemed to be no tension there.

Sister Mary Joseph wore a black and white habit. All you could see of her body was her face, a little bit of dark hair on her forehead, a little of her neck, and her hands from the wrists down, which were very different from my mother's and mine. Her skin was very white, and she wore no polish on her clean nails. One day I asked Sister Mary Joseph about the gold ring she wore on her left hand. She explained that it was a wedding band, and that she was married to God. I decided that she must be special if she was married to God. I looked at her all the time and watched her expressions. Parts of me were always checking to see whether her face had the scary expressions I saw at home. I never saw scary looks on her face, but I never stopped looking.

Sister Mary Joseph showed me a classroom in the convent where I would take lessons in reading and writing Spanish from some nuns from South America. My mom had already cleared it with my father, who seemed pleased with the idea. Many days that fall, I stayed at the convent until my mom finished work and came by so we could walk home together. Some days she smiled, held my hand as we walked, and asked me about my day. Other days she had a blank expression and we walked home next to each other but as if alone, not touching or talking. Either way, when we got home I tried to go up to my room as quickly and quietly as I could. But if my father was nearby, he'd call me over and quiz me about my Spanish lessons to make sure the nuns and I were doing what we said we would.

One day Sister Mary Joseph brought in a Bible as a gift for me and we started reading it after school together—or, rather, we looked at the pictures and talked about the stories. She looked at me with such kindness and care when we sat together at her desk and talked about the Bible. I tried to hold on to the feeling of being close to her—her kind smile, her caring eyes. I was the only student with whom she was reading the Bible. *She must care about me.* I closed my fist to capture those thoughts in the part that held all the special things Sister Mary Joseph did and said.

At times, though, I must have been very challenging for her. My levels of anxiety ebbed and flowed that year. I did well in school, but I had trouble concentrating and loved to talk and make people laugh. Of course, Sister Mary Joseph had a class to teach, and I made it harder for her to maintain order. I started that school year in a seat in the back row. After she noticed that I talked straight through her lessons, she moved me to the front of the class. But that didn't stop me from talking to the kids sitting next to me. Exasperated, she situated my little desk next to her big desk only to discover, much to her dismay, that I would then talk to her. Finally, Sister Mary Joseph put my desk in a corner in the front of the room, away from everyone else. From there I occasionally made comments to the entire class, but mostly I was quiet, so I stayed there most of the year. Still, Sister Mary Joseph paid close attention to me. Whenever I raised my hand she called on me, and she often praised me for my answers. I felt special and smart, like someone who was worth noticing.

The abuse at home got worse that year and challenged my internal coping mechanisms. My father sexually abused me anytime he and I were alone in the house together. If I came home from school and we were alone, a part of me routinely took over and, in unbearable anxious anticipation of a rape, found my father and initiated the abuse. If I saw a particular look on his face or sensed menace in his step, a door opened in my mind and a part came forward to deal with the trigger. My father regularly appeared in my room at night, waking me by clasping his hand over my mouth and sliding into bed. At these times, too, a part would come forward to accommodate what he had wanted me to do in the past.

Perhaps the abuse increased because my father was losing control over our family. Mike started playing football, grew very close to his coach, and spent less and less time at home. When Mike was home, he was distant in the way my mom was. He ignored all of us and stopped playing with me. My mother's job kept her later and later into the evenings. My father accused her of having affairs with men at work. He accused Mike of being disrespectful to him. And he watched Alex closely, catching all of his missteps. My father seemed to hate all of us and was enraged almost all the time at one offense or another. We all tried to tread very lightly the year I was in second grade.

I constantly watched my father's face, listened to the tones in his voice, and watched his mannerisms. I was increasingly nervous at home and, when I could, spent most of my time in my room sitting in a corner under the bathroom window or curled up under my bed. A calmer feeling often came over me when I felt my back against the wall. My eyes shifted from side to side and my thoughts raced: *Does Sister Mary Joseph really like me? I must be her favorite. She doesn't keep anyone else after school. We go to the convent together. The nuns are so nice. I wish I could live there. Am I too young to be married to God?* A part of me that idolized Sister Mary Joseph and the nuns in the convent came closer to the surface and I felt happy. I raised a fist to my ear to hear the wonderful voices of the nuns. I could feel their hugs as I greeted them. I saw myself in my white habit, all pressed and clean, holding their hands and praying. We skipped and glided and played in the playground at my school.

One night that winter my father woke me in his usual manner. I panicked and started to go deep inside to allow the part of me that responded to his abuse to come forward. But I saw that he was smiling. His eyes bulged and he laughed with an eerie edge that I hadn't heard before. Then, just past him I saw Mike and Alex. At first I was relieved, thinking that they were finally going to help me, that maybe they could stop him. I came back closer to the surface but quickly realized they were only in my room because Popi made them come in. They both looked meek and confused.

My father pulled the covers off me and began to rape me. He gestured for my brothers to come closer. My body was cold and full of fear. My ears throbbed with rushing blood, so I couldn't hear what my father was saying, but I understood that he was going to instruct them in how to rape me. I felt like my head was going to burst and I was going to jump out of my skin until, as so many times before, my mind mercifully took over. I became numb and my panic eased. I was in my shell, hovering on the ceiling, watching someone else's family.

This was an attack on all of us. Step-by-step my father showed Mike and Alex what to do. He showed them how I made it easy by not fighting back. He explained that my stillness meant that I wanted it. He made both of my brothers rape me that night. I split off again and again. One part formed to capture the look on my father's face, other parts captured my brothers' expressions, another captured the feel of their grip on my arms, other parts took the physical pain, and still others took the humiliation.

In the hours the attack lasted, I created twenty to thirty parts or fragments of parts—interconnected rooms, each holding only a tiny bit of this new devastation. This way, if for some reason I stumbled upon a piece of information, or one room, I wouldn't remember the whole of what was happening. At that time, I couldn't have known the whole of it and survived. I developed many parts to contain what happened that night and the subsequent nights that my father made my brothers rape me.

The fuzzy feeling in my head grew deeper, which made it possible for another part to come forward and soothe me even while I was being attacked. For the first time, as other parts of me absorbed and whisked away details of the attack, I left the scene altogether and escaped into my well-rehearsed fantasy. I was in the convent living among the nuns, and we were playing games. One nun told me I was the smartest girl she had ever met. Another said I was very special. Another told me that God loved me. Sister Mary Joseph held a Bible as we read together. Doña Graciela, at the convent for a visit, led us all in prayer: "Hail Mary, full of grace…"

4

ame explained to my brothers and me that she and Popi were treating me to a "special night" out. I was excited. *But why was I being treated to something special?* In protest, my brothers asked the exact question that I was thinking. My father responded in a warning tone, "She's the only girl, so she gets a special night." His tone was clear. My brothers didn't say another word.

I didn't have a lot of dresses that fit. My favorite was a white lace dress that fit fine up top but was really too short. I put on the white socks and black patent leather shoes that were only for church and special occasions. But when we arrived at our destination, the look on my mother's face gave me the idea that this was no ordinary social visit. She was often distant and irritated, but this look was different. Her face seemed cold and hard, like she was bracing herself for something. It was similar to how she looked after my father hit her and she knew he was about to do it again. Her face scared me and my thoughts started to race: *What's happening? Where are we? Whose house is this?* I searched my father for a sign. He looked different too, and I couldn't figure it out. I tried to calm myself.

My mom told me harshly to get out of the car. *This doesn't feel like a special night.* My heart started to pound harder as we approached the house. A sense of panic crept in when a man opened the door and looked me over, but soon a familiar calm took its place. My father introduced the man to me as Mr. Smith.

Once we entered the house, my mom sat stony faced in the living room while my father ushered me into the bedroom behind Mr. Smith. Mr. Smith spoke to me in a childishly sweet voice, telling me how fun the bed was to jump on, then saying, "Try it out." I panicked again and told Mr. Smith that I didn't want to. I looked to Popi but could tell by his face that I wasn't allowed to say no, and if I did, there would be consequences. Popi picked me up and threw me on the bed. Mr. Smith slapped me and held me down, but I fought hard—hitting, biting, and kicking Mr. Smith wherever I thought it could hurt. I screamed, *"No!"* Then I heard and felt my father strike me with his belt. I'm sure he was surprised by my reaction, since I hadn't fought my brothers and it had been a long time since I had fought him. But this was different. I didn't know this man or his home. My father had always told me that what he did to me at home was my fault. But somehow I knew this was not my fault, and I wasn't going to obey.

I wet my pants and vomited on the bed. Mr. Smith angrily told my father that he wasn't going to pay. Once I heard this I relaxed, thinking I had won and we would now go home. But I was wrong. As soon as I stopped fighting, Mr. Smith unzipped his pants. I panicked again. A part of me knew that I couldn't win. My head filled with cotton. I left my body for the safety of the ceiling and watched Mr. Smith rape me. I noticed that my father stayed in the room and watched as well. When Mr. Smith was done with me, he left me on the bed and he and my father walked out and argued about whether Mr. Smith should have to pay. In the end, Mr. Smith refused. I got up in my usual daze and used a towel from the bathroom to clean myself off. My parents escorted me out of the house and back to the car.

My father yelled at me all the way home. When we got there, my mother went silently to their bedroom and my father took me into my room, past my brothers pretending to be asleep in their beds. Angrily, he said, "We need the money for food and for rent, Olguita! You've ruined it. Now we can't pay the rent."

"What about Mom's job and the money she brings home?"

He hit my face hard and I fell to the floor. "Don't disrespect me. And don't ever fight like that again. You do what I tell you to do." I could feel the beginning of his hand mark coming up on my face and thought, *I hate you, Popi. I wish you would die.* That night when he raped me, he told me, "You are mine, Olguita. Don't ever forget: You were mine first."

For several years, my parents and I had special nights like these every week. We would visit my father's friends and acquaintances in the Latino community, and because I had no complete memory of the past, I was excited each time, putting on my best clothes again and hopping in the car. But as soon as I saw that cold, hard look on my mom's face, it triggered memories of when this had happened before, and the part came forward that knew we were going to some man's house so he could do bad things to me and pay my father for it. This part was angry and refused to stop fighting back. I didn't care that my father hit me. I wanted to be hit so hard that I'd be knocked out and never wake up.

My resistance was a big problem for my parents, who often weren't paid when I fought back. Thinking that alcohol would make me more submissive, my mother started making me drink a glass of whiskey when we arrived at the houses. When one glass didn't calm me the way they had hoped, she forced me to drink another. My adrenaline must have been so high that the first glass barely touched it, but the second glass always worked. This ended up being the best strategy.

This worked so well that my mother began giving me a glass or two of wine at home before we even left or as soon as I got in the car. If I was triggered by being offered alcohol and resisted drinking it, she'd try to be persuasive: "Olguita, you need to do this. We need money for food and to stay in our house." This explanation, giving me the responsibility for supporting my family, was powerful and effective. I didn't want our family to have to move out of our house. I didn't want our family to go hungry. So I complied.

I clearly remember my early resistance, fighting as hard as my little body could and arguing with my mom about drinking the wine. But I have little memory of the rapes that occurred after I drank enough to be subdued. I mainly remember the pain in my body afterward and the pain my father inflicted on me when we got home, always telling me, "You are mine, and no one else's," as he raped me.

To survive I created more and more parts, interconnected rooms to store pieces of the memories so that I wouldn't have to fully realize that my parents prostituted me for years. I even created a set of parts to commit suicide if I ever did stumble across a memory of what had been done to me. The rooms holding the information about the prostitution were separated by rooms that held suicidal plans. It was a rudimentary strategy, effective at the time but ultimately dangerous to me in a new way. Many years later, when I did start to piece everything together, I often felt a compelling need to die from the despair.

• • •

From the corner of my parent's bedroom, I watched my mother throwing things, mostly my father's clothes. She must have known it would upset him, because he was always so meticulous. But she didn't seem to care. She was angrier than I had ever seen her. After the rage settled, my mom fell on her bed and cried. I went over to comfort her, but she didn't respond. A few minutes later she suddenly stopped crying and became cold and hard.

Earlier that morning, a stranger had come by the house to evict us. He said that he was sorry, but we would have to leave. It turned out that my father had spent most of the money he earned prostituting me on new suits, ties, and hats and had been regularly skipping rent payments. He had spent the money however he wanted, just as he did with my mother's salary.

Later, when my father got home, I listened from the hall closet upstairs as my mother confronted him in the kitchen: "How can it be that I give you all the money I make at work and all the money we make with Olguita and you do not pay the rent for a year! What do you do with this money?"

"I am the man here, and I can do what I want with my money!" I heard a dish shatter. My father must have thrown it for emphasis.

"Alejandro," came my mother's voice, now a bit softer, "what are we going to do this time? We'll have to take the kids out of school. No one around here will rent us a house."

Popi sounded indifferent. "Then we'll move downtown. They can go to public school. They are better there anyway." I knew my father didn't really feel this way, but he always refused to admit any wrongdoing. From my hiding place in the dark, my sense of panic about moving again was taken over by a numbness that I had come to rely on. They argued for what felt like hours, and over that time I heard my mom's voice go from angry to controlled disgust to a flat monotone. I had never heard my mother have such utter disdain for my father. He was at times indignant, and I heard more dishes break, but mostly he seemed unconcerned. I sat in the closet with my rosary, praying. I rubbed the beads and thought of Doña Graciela. My parents' relationship was never the same. Mame rarely talked to Popi after that night.

●　●　●

Soon after that night, the spring of the year I turned eleven, we moved into an apartment downtown that my mom had found. This move marked a shift in my mom, who went away inside to a degree I hadn't seen before. She seemed cold and angry all the way through. The move marked a shift for me, too. I started doing a lot of the cleaning and cooking for the family. I didn't want to, but a few days after we moved in my mom came to my room and sat with me, and not in the way she had earlier, when she would come to my room to talk to me about a change in our lives. She didn't hold my hand. There wasn't any of the tenderness she had shown when I was younger.

"Olguita, I've been promoted at work. I'll make more money, but I have to work more hours." I listened quietly but thought, *I don't believe you. You are going to spend time with Tomás.* Tomás was my mother's boss, and I had begun to wonder if they were having an affair.

My suspicions had started one summer a couple of years before, when Popi went away to visit his family in Bolivia. At least, that's where he said he was going. The trip came as a big surprise to us because Popi never talked about his family. All he'd ever told us was that he ran away from home when he was very young. My brothers and I weren't invited along on the trip, even though we had never met our grandparents on his side of the family and weren't in school.

When Popi was away that summer, Tomás came over quite a bit. He'd always driven my mom back and forth to work, but this felt different. I came home one day and was surprised to find Tomás's car parked on the side street and my mom home early. I called out for my mom and heard talking upstairs, then my mom came down, straightening her dress. Her hair was messy and she looked surprised and guilty, like she had been caught doing something. A few minutes later Tomás came down the stairs and announced that the curtains upstairs were very nice. "Thank you for showing them to me. I think that's what we will need in our apartment." At the time, I didn't understand what was happening, but I could sense that my mom was doing something she didn't want anyone to know about.

Now, as my mom and I sat in my bedroom in the new apartment, my mom said, "I need your help, Olguita. When I'm working late, I need you to clean the apartment and cook dinner for your brothers and your father. I'll show you how. It's easy." And with that, she walked out of my room. Inside, I could feel anger rising. *Why do I have to do everything? What about Mike and Alex?* But I sat silently as the anger filled me, and suddenly a familiar, numb feeling came over me and calmed me.

From that day forward, I came home from school, did my homework, cleaned the apartment, and cooked dinner for my father and brothers. I wasn't ever very good at cooking and never wanted to get any better. *If they don't like it, that's too bad. Let them make their own dinner.*

Anger wasn't a safe emotion for me to express in our home. I hated my father, Alex, and Mike, but I could never say so or I would surely be beaten. As I look back on it now, my mom's emotional departure from our family, and how she left me to keep house and make dinner for my father and brothers, was the last straw. Somewhere inside, among my many parts, there was an accounting of everything that had been done to me. I didn't remember the specifics, but I must have had an idea that a serious injustice had occurred, because being told that I was expected to take care of my father and brothers raised a fury in me that I could not contain. But since I couldn't safely express it, new parts of me developed to hold the anger and rage. Already a budding athlete, I began playing sports even more aggressively, and as I grew older I vented the anger by running and lifting weights compulsively. I now know that many of my feelings of extreme hopelessness and suicidal thoughts also came from the rage I could never express.

● ● ●

That fall, I came home from fifth grade to find my mom home early, rushing around gathering up some of my father's belongings. I was confused and frightened by the urgency in her movements. She explained, "Olguita, your father had a heart attack today and he could die. He is in the hospital and I have to go there right away."

The recent changes in our lives—a new school, a new home, and a new set of teachers and friends—had already challenged the delicate balance of parts that helped me survive. My world was threatening to change again, and I couldn't bear it. *Heart attack. He could die.* This time when the panic subsided, the usual numbness was joined by strange feelings: a separation more dramatic than ever before. It didn't start in my hands. It felt like my head was literally breaking apart. A sharp headache started, then I had a feeling of being very far away, or very small in a large world. This was different from anything I'd felt before. My thoughts weren't racing, and I wasn't anxious. Instead, my thoughts slowly went from being sad for my father to being afraid of what would happen next to being happy that he was gone. The parts inside were deeply conflicted, and my thoughts were slow and pondering. I could feel them but didn't understand them. As my mom told me that my father could die, I heard her as if I was at the end of a very long tunnel. My inner world began to fall in on itself.

I sat quietly, frustrated by the fact that I could barely think. *I'm taking too long. I can't figure out how to feel about this.* The conflict inside became stronger and my headache got worse. *I'm taking too long! Stop! How am I supposed to feel? What do I say?* My mom stopped collecting my father's things and looked at me for a second. I searched her eyes for some sense of how she was feeling in an effort to figure out how I should feel. I saw a flat stare that quickly turned to annoyance that I was keeping her. She resumed her hurried search. Finally, I asked, "What about Alex and Mike? Are you going to tell them?" My brothers weren't home from school yet.

"I don't have time," Mame said. "A friend is waiting downstairs to drive me to the hospital. You'll have to tell them. I'll be home late. Don't wait up." And out she went. Mostly numb and with a little bit of fear, I sat in a daze and waited for my brothers.

As I served Alex and Mike dinner that night, I watched them closely for some clue of how to feel. They mostly complained about the food. Anger rose inside me. *You cook, then!* Eventually we put ourselves to bed. My mom got home very late. Looking exhausted, she woke us up to talk about Popi.

"Did Popi die?" I asked her.

"No, Olguita." She seemed annoyed at the question. She told us that Popi had a massive heart attack and was in intensive care. They wouldn't know for a while whether he would be okay. He could still die. I searched for emotion behind her words, but there was none. I looked at my brothers. They were flat too. Inside I was numb. I didn't feel sad anymore. I didn't feel scared, either. I felt nothing.

● ○ ●

My father survived the heart attack, and several weeks later the doctors sent him home to recuperate. My after-school chores turned into a full-time job. Since Mame had to go to work, I stayed home from school to take care of him. After all, who would stay home with him if I didn't? My mother said she couldn't because she'd get fired. But I knew better. Because she was having an affair with her boss, he wouldn't fire her. I didn't feel anything for Popi at this point. I didn't want to stay home and take care of him; I wanted to be in school with my friends. I was a crossing guard, and I was afraid I'd lose my corner. I worried about getting behind in my schoolwork. My teachers were kind enough to send my assignments home, but I had trouble concentrating, so I usually wasn't able to do them. I had always learned best by listening to and watching my teachers.

The first day I stayed home with my father, I stood in the kitchen door and watched him sitting in the living room, assessing him. We were about to spend many long days together alone. He didn't look like the man I had known all my life. Wearing only pajamas, he sat and stared off into space. Before his heart attack, he never would have left his bedroom without being carefully dressed and groomed. But he didn't seem to care anymore. He was just staring, and his stare didn't seem to fall on anything in particular. When he did focus on me, he looked sad. *He doesn't look like Popi anymore. He's so sad and weak. Will he die in front of me? What do I do if he dies?* Before his heart attack he had always been very animated, avidly reading the newspaper, watching TV, or talking to me about politics. But now he simply stared at the TV, which was off, and his newspapers sat next to him unread. It was a beautiful fall day, and behind him a big picture window overlooked a small playground and basketball court, but he was uninterested.

As I looked closer, I could see tears streaming down his face. I had never seen my father cry before. It startled me and I thought, *He's scared. He's dying. He's all alone.* I watched him without saying a word. I didn't ask him why he was crying or try to distract him from his grief with a TV show or a game of dominos. I just stood there, quiet and distant. I was wary of him but not really afraid. He didn't seem able to physically hurt me anymore, but I wondered if somehow he would still try. *He's not so scary now. He can't hurt me anymore.* He looked like a shell of himself, crumpled in his chair. My thoughts shifted again. *What's going to happen to him? What's going to happen to me?*

He still wanted eggs and bacon for breakfast, but he wasn't supposed to eat that anymore, and he was no longer in charge. My mom said he was on a low-fat diet. I served him a bowl of puffed wheat cereal with low-fat milk. He looked at it with his same stare and then ate it slowly. From the kitchen, I heard him complain about how tasteless the cereal was. Slowly it occurred to me that I had just defied my father. I had told him he couldn't eat what he wanted and I hadn't gotten hurt. *See, he isn't able to hurt me anymore.*

After about a week of this, I realized that I wasn't so nervous around my father. I started talking to him more directly. At first I was a little unsure but gradually became braver. I started turning on the TV and talking to Popi about politics. He became a little livelier. We got into a habit of sitting together and watching the news. He began to read his papers again and told me about what was happening in his beloved South America. Although I became more comfortable around him, I never developed a sense of love or even fondness for my father. I never stopped feeling cold and distant inside. Numb was all he had trained me to be.

As my father's vigor returned, he complained more and more vocally about his diet. Our conversation also strayed into frightening topics: "Your mother doesn't love me. You know she's not really working late. She is with Tomás. I've lost her." My thoughts raced for the first time in weeks: *He knows. He'll kill her. He'll kill all of us.* "Your brothers don't love me either. They don't respect me." My brothers had been spending even less time at our apartment now that my father was home all the time. "You're the only one who loves me." As he spoke, I saw only sadness in his face, none of the rage that usually came with topics like disrespect. He felt abandoned. I calmed myself and my thoughts switched. *He can't hurt me anymore.* I sat there quietly. I couldn't feel any love for him, but I listened.

He asked me to go to his bedroom and get a leather box out of his dresser drawer. I found it and brought it to him. He looked inside the box and then looked at me. He was crying. One by one, he pulled out the small items in the box and described each to me: an American fifty-cent piece, a Hubert H. Humphrey campaign button from 1968, a pair of cufflinks, and a tiny box with my baby teeth in it. He was crying even harder now. Something seemed wrong but I couldn't figure it out. I got scared and then felt numb. My father gave the box to me and thanked me for taking care of him. I didn't say a word. Later that evening, when my mom got home from work, I pulled her aside and told her about the box. The next morning she sent me back to school and took my father to the hospital. She said he was getting worse.

Just a few days later, Tomás came into the apartment after driving my mom home. It was Halloween and I was home alone doing my chores. My mom sat next to Tomás on the couch, holding his hand, as he told me that Popi had died. I was instantly confused and didn't understand his words. *Popi died? Popi died? What is "died"?* Then I looked at Tomás in anger. *Who is this man to me? Why is he telling me?* Then my thoughts shifted again. I looked at my mom, who was silently staring at her lap. I willed her to look up at me, but she didn't. *Why isn't she talking to me?* I tried hard to figure out what all of this meant. I didn't know how to feel. My thoughts shifted again. *If I could see her eyes, I would know how to feel.* She didn't appear to be crying. She was just staring at her hand in Tomás's larger one. I stared at their hands too.

Tomás was older than my mom but not as old as Popi. He looked a lot like Popi: He had a small stature, was balding, and had a small mustache. He dressed well too, in a suit and tie with a fedora-type hat. But Tomás had a job, and he seemed kinder than Popi. He was kind to my mom and normally I liked that about him, but now I was angry that he was here telling me about Popi dying. Then all of a sudden, it struck me: Popi was dead and would never be coming back. I felt calm and very relieved.

I asked my mom, "Can I go trick-or-treating tonight?"

She responded mechanically, the first time she had spoken: "No, it's disrespectful. You will stay home tonight, and you'll be staying home from school this week too." She didn't look sad. She didn't look anything.

In a flat tone, she started talking about the wake and the funeral, listing aloud all the things that needed to be done. Her stare was deep and I couldn't tell who she was talking to. "We have to call the church. We need to find a funeral home. We have to call my sisters and brother. We need to get his things out of here." Then in a flash her worry deepened, her voice raised, and she turned to Tomás and said, "We don't have any money. How will we pay for this?"

I watched and listened as they talked to each other, my mom panicky and Tomás in a caring, supportive voice. Worry seemed to be overtaking her. The increasing tension in her voice scared me and something shifted inside. *She's really scared.* The thoughts came faster as my own fear increased. *What do I do? How do I help?* Hesitantly, I said, "We'll be okay, Mame." She stopped talking to Tomás and shot me an angry look, and I withdrew again.

Now I recognize that we were coping in similar ways. At a time when many women would feel overwhelming grief at losing a husband, or overwhelming relief at losing an abusive spouse, my mom was going back and forth between numbness and obsessive worry, just as I had always done. I was relieved that my father wouldn't be coming back, but also afraid of what would happen to us. I was desperate to have someone tell me what my next day, week, and month were going to be like—what my life was going to be like. I needed order and stability, and despite my feeling of relief at my father's death, my future seemed uncertain and frightening. I didn't know why then, but I had good reason to be afraid.

Unnoticed by my mom and Tomás, I went to my room and sat on my bed. I knew that to show respect for my father I wasn't supposed to have fun, laugh, or play, so I crawled into the corner of my room and sat there quietly. I felt safe there, calmer. I let my eyes become unfocused and let my thoughts race without trying to catch them. I sat there quietly for the rest of the evening, listening to my mom telling my brothers about Popi and hearing her calling her family, our church, and our next-door neighbors to let them know my father was dead.

That weekend my aunts, uncles, and cousins from my mom's side of the family came for the wake and the funeral. It was nice to see them. They always treated me with love and affection. Mame asked them to help her collect all of my father's belongings, put them in bags and boxes, and give them away. After the funeral they stayed to visit with her coworkers and friends, and eventually left with everything of my father's except the box of trinkets he had given me and an old photo album. The photos showed him in his twenties and thirties, smiling and laughing with friends, usually smoking a cigar.

We weren't in those pictures. He didn't look like the man I knew. Later, I studied his smile and the look in his eyes and wondered what he was like before he met my mother and before we kids were born. I never saw that kind of smile on him. *Why was he so happy then? Why wasn't he happy with us?*

My mom's family seemed to be fully aware of how my father had treated her. When she asked them to take away everything that had been his, no one seemed surprised and no questions were asked. As I watched them pack up his clothes, I heard them comment on how nice and expensive his suits were. I felt a surge of anger, but I didn't know why. Most of that week I was numb. But somewhere inside there was relief, and somewhere else there was the fear of not knowing what to expect. I hoped desperately to finally have my mother back, the loving, caring woman I adored.

However, during the weeks and months that followed, Mame's worries grew. Over and over again she'd say, "How will I provide for you? How will I do this on my own?" Her worries made no sense to me. After all, she had been providing for the five of us for years, and now we wouldn't have my father spending all her money any way he pleased. I kept offering her my standard response: that we would be okay, and that she was already taking care of us just fine. But it was as if she couldn't see or hear me. I felt helpless. I so desperately wanted her attention and love. I had thought that now that Popi was gone she would come back to me. I'd thought she would go back to being the loving mom who held my hand and put a smiley face in the "O" on my lunch bag.

Instead, my mom's worry spun more and more into a way of being. She worried about work. She worried about Alex's delinquent behavior. She worried about Mike's insolent attitude and gradual disappearance from our home. And her worries became my worries: *Would she get fired? Would she be able to support us? Why was Mike so rude to her?*

Years before, a part of me had formed to intervene protectively when I saw my father beating my mother. It tried to comfort her sadness and pain after Popi hurt her. Later, that part would come forward when I was with her in public and saw people lose patience because they couldn't understand her English through her thick Dominican accent. But now, with all the worry and change in our lives, the part that protected my mom couldn't grapple with every problem or threat to her without becoming overwhelmed. My mom's worries had become so vast that this protective part had to split off into many parts that could focus on different worries and try to take care of them for her.

I suppressed the parts that were angry with her for prostituting me and the parts that felt abandoned by her when she withdrew so far into herself. Instead, one part made sure I behaved well. I always did what I was told and never talked back or argued. Another part formed to make sure the apartment was always clean. Another cooked. A part formed to get babysitting jobs so my mother wouldn't worry so much about money. But the most persistent part was one that kept reaching out to get Mame to come back.

Learning to See
in the Dark

5

The summer I turned twelve, I spent every available minute at the pool. Every day from June through August I got up early, did the chores my mother asked me to do, and tried to be at the pool by the time it opened. I stayed until it closed if I could, taking the short walk home to our apartment just in time to make dinner.

Despite how much time I spent at the pool, I couldn't swim. I mostly just waded in the shallower end of the pool with the younger kids. I was embarrassed to be so old and not be able to swim, especially since it seemed that kids half my age could swim easily. I was constantly in fear of having older kids at the pool or my brothers make fun of me. I already felt stupid, ugly, and dirty, and I wanted to disappear. I didn't know then where my enormous sense of shame came from. I didn't even understand that not everyone felt this way.

A friend of mine from the apartment building, Eleanor, tried to teach me to swim, but there wasn't a whole lot to her lessons. Mostly she swam around and then said, "Now you do that." When I tried, the thought of learning how to swim in front of older kids or my brothers sent me into a panic and I simply couldn't copy her.

One day she changed her approach and tried to break swimming down into steps: "You have to pick up your feet, close your eyes, and move your arms and legs like this." I carefully watched Eleanor move her arms in a wide circle and flutter kick her feet and wished I could do that so easily. I looked around to see who was watching. The rest of the kids were playing and swimming, and no one was looking at me. I picked up my feet and immediately sank to the bottom of the pool. I panicked and thrashed around, then finally got my feet back underneath me and stood up. I felt stupid. After a couple of tries, I gave up. But Eleanor was always upbeat about our lessons. "We'll try again tomorrow."

One day I noticed that one of the lifeguards, Liz, was watching my efforts. When I caught her eye, she smiled and moved her arms in the same way Eleanor had. Later, when I was sunbathing in a pool chair, Liz got out of her lifeguard chair and came over to me. "Olga?" I wondered how she knew my name, but then remembered we had to have an apartment pass to use the pool. Sometimes she was the one I handed my pass to. "I could teach you how to swim if you'd like. You could come an hour before the pool opens. It would just be you and me, and I could show you."

My heart raced and I couldn't get the words out to respond. All sorts of thoughts spun around in my head: *Liz came over to talk to me. She's in college and really cool. She could teach me to swim—without anyone seeing how stupid I am.* Finally I just said, "That would be great. Thank you."

Every morning for the next few weeks, I got to the pool an hour before it opened. Liz taught me how to move my arms, hold my hands, and kick my feet. While I practiced kicking, she held me so I wouldn't sink to the bottom of the pool and panic. I trusted Liz. "Close your eyes and blow out through your nose. You don't want to swallow any water." I felt more and more capable and accomplished as I learned how to swim. I held on to the feeling, closed my fist around it, and felt a gentle separation inside me as another part was created that could swim and be Liz's friend. This splitting happened frequently now, creating more parts that could hold on to good, positive feelings to counter the bad feelings inside.

There was a time when I would have shared my excitement over these successes with my mom, but it had been years since I had told her about my triumphs, and she didn't ask. Liz was different. She was eighteen years old and like an older sister. I felt comfortable talking with her, and she listened. She taught me that I could learn to do new things and that I could solve problems. That summer and for the next few years of our friendship, my worry and obsessive thinking focused on Liz. I woke up in the morning and went over my most recent interactions with Liz to see if I'd said or done something stupid. I reviewed every word I'd spoken, how she looked at me, and what she said, and wondered if she still liked me. Although this was very painful, my worry and obsessive thinking about Liz helped me avoid thinking about the way my brothers, now teenagers, had picked up abusing me where my father left off.

• • •

On my twelfth birthday that summer, near the end of June, I finished my morning swimming lesson with Liz and ran back home to do laundry for my mom. We didn't have a washer and dryer in our apartment, so we used the shared ones in the basement of the building. The dirty clothes bin was full and I knew I would have to do at least three loads. My mom had left me with a list of chores to do while she was at work, and I was sad and frustrated because she didn't seem to remember that it was my birthday.

My brother Alex was with his friend Gary in the basement storage area. Alex had made an empty storage compartment into a clubhouse, and he and his friends often hung out down there, reading *Playboy* magazines and smoking pot. It was a good place for a club because not many people came through the storage area. As I started the first load washing, I heard Alex and Gary calling me. They said they wanted to show me something. I was curious, but as I got near the clubhouse, I smelled pot and started to get uneasy. I could hear them speaking softly: "...thinks she's so special on her birthday. Let's teach her a lesson." In his own twisted fashion, Alex had grown to deeply resent what he saw as my father's preferential treatment of me, back when Popi was alive. Alex had often made me pay for my "special nights" with taunting and beatings the next day when my father wasn't around. Even though I didn't have those specific memories that day, when I heard him sneeringly call me "special" something clicked inside me and I felt fear.

Too late, I turned to run back upstairs, but Alex caught me and threw me into the storage compartment. My head rushed with blood and everything sounded muffled. My eyes shifted back and forth quickly, and then a part of me that hated Alex came forward and fought back. I yelled, "I hate you!" with all the rage I had inside me and swung my fists wildly but hardly hurt him. I kicked his legs and screamed, cursing. I spit at his face and then lunged forward to bite him on the arm. That hurt him, and I was glad.

Alex was bigger and stronger than I was, though, and he didn't have much trouble grabbing me in a bear hug with my arms pinned. He threw me up against the concrete wall of the storage room, and then picked me up and did it again and again until I fell to the ground unconscious. When I came to, Alex was raping me. I first felt an intense sense of panic, but instinctively my mind reacted to save me and my head filled with cotton. The panic went away and I felt calm. I separated from my body and went up to the ceiling to watch Alex and Gary take turns raping someone who looked like me but didn't feel like me. When they were done, they both urinated on me. I didn't move. "See, Gary? She'll let you do anything to her. She's such a whore." Their attack had felt endless and I wanted to die.

I later discovered that during the attack a part of me formed to keep this new level of humiliation and violence away from me, absorb the experience of the attack, and try to get me out of harm's way. I now think of her as Twelve. After Alex and Gary left, I came back into my body, and while this new part stayed present I slowly got up in a daze. She knew the basement was no longer a safe place, so she stayed close to the surface as I looked at my torn clothes and felt the pain and wetness from what Alex and Gary had done. I was filled with shame and didn't want anyone to see me. *I have to get out of here.* Although this thought was compelling and strong, there were conflicting thoughts running through my head: *But Mom says I can't leave the laundry down in the basement.* The internal debate didn't last long. I panicked at the idea of staying in the basement, so I held my ripped clothes on me with one hand as I gathered the clothes out of the washer. I used the basket of wet clothes to cover myself up so no one would see the rips and stains in my clothes and then walked in slow motion up the three flights of stairs to our apartment.

When I reached the door, I felt numb. Then another compelling thought raced through my mind: *Alex hurt me badly, and I could still be in danger.* I was overtaken by a surge of fear: *What if Alex is in there?* I stood in the hallway in front of our apartment door for a couple of minutes, stuck between the numbness and the fear. Then I pushed forward through the daze and went quietly inside and directly to my room while looking around to see if anyone was home. No one was. I picked out clean clothes, peered out my door to double-check whether anyone was around, and then scurried to the bathroom to clean the blood, semen, and urine from my body. The parts of me that had learned to clean up all those years ago came forward to comfort me with the ritual. As I became calmer, the compelling thoughts that were so strong went further away, taking my memory of the attack into a locked room inside my mind.

I stayed far away in my head, with a deep fuzziness that left me feeling nothing. I couldn't focus my eyes. I felt withdrawn and all alone. I threw the ripped and stained clothes away, picked up the wet clothes I had washed earlier and another load of laundry, and returned to the basement. I sat on the floor in the corner of the laundry room, staring at nothing in particular, as I waited for the next load of clothes to wash and then dry. I packed up the two loads and went back up to my bedroom and closed the door, exhausted. I didn't finish the laundry or the other chores on my list. I didn't go back to the pool that day even though I'd told Liz that I would. I just sat in the corner between my bed and the wall with my numb, unfocused stare, which only deepened when I heard voices in the apartment.

When my mom came home and noticed that I hadn't finished my chores, she asked, "Olga, what have you been doing today? You didn't wash the dishes, you didn't make dinner, and the laundry is only partly done. What is wrong with you? I've worked all day and you cannot do some simple chores to help me?" My heart sank as I heard the bitterness in her voice. She didn't remember my birthday. I finished the laundry and washed the dishes as she cooked dinner— our typical fare of black beans and rice. I felt bad for disappointing her and adding to her list of worries. I doubted myself: *Is she right that she can't count on me? Am I as bad as my brothers for not helping her?*

I went to bed early that night, still feeling the fuzziness that helped me stay numb. I didn't remember the attack and couldn't have told my mom or anyone else even if I'd wanted to. With Twelve now in her own room in the house inside me, I felt anxiety whenever I was around Alex, but I didn't consciously know why he was dangerous, nor did I realize that his friend Gary now knew he could rape me and I wouldn't tell anyone. I could only tell that for some reason Gary unnerved me and I should avoid him. But he proved to be relentless, seeking me out over and over again.

● ● ●

The next day I went to the pool early again, but I was quiet and withdrawn. Although I didn't know why, I felt so bad about myself that I couldn't look Liz in the eyes. I didn't remember the attack. I just felt ugly, fat, and awful. "What's wrong? Why didn't you come back yesterday, like you said you would? And where did you get these scrapes and bruises?"

I was stunned. "What scrapes and bruises?" I searched my memory for what had happened the previous day, why I didn't come back to the pool and how I'd gotten hurt, but I couldn't remember. My head started getting fuzzy and I stared vacantly at the ground. Liz searched my eyes and then changed the subject.

"Hey, so I heard yesterday was your birthday." I was excited that she knew and remembered. "I was going to take you to Bob's Big Boy for some strawberry shortcake for your birthday. Do you want to go today instead?"

My eyes lit up. "Really? I would love to go!"

"When I'm done with my shift, we'll change and I'll take you." I thought about it all day. At first my mind was full of excitement: *I'm going to Bob's Big Boy with Liz. I'm special. I get to ride in her car.* But soon my thoughts turned from excitement to worry: *What if I do something stupid? What if she changes her mind? What if she sees how awful I am? I hope I don't do anything wrong.* Then I worried even more: *What will I say? What is Bob's Big Boy? Will my clothes be okay?*

Bob's Big Boy turned out to be a diner-style restaurant that served burgers, sandwiches, and pies. It was my first time eating strawberry shortcake and drinking Earl Grey tea, which I ordered because Liz did. She asked for extra whipped cream on her strawberry shortcake, so I did too. I wanted to be just like her. I must have stared at her all evening with a big smile on my face.

It was magical being with her. She looked at me and talked to me like no one ever had before. She asked me question after question: "What do you like to do?"

"I don't know."

"Do you like going to the movies?"

"The only two movies I've seen are *Ben Hur* and *Oliver*."

"Oh, we'll fix that. I love the movies, especially science fiction and suspense movies. Would you like to go sometime?"

"*Yes!* I would love to," I blurted out so loudly that heads turned in the restaurant. Liz acted like she didn't even notice.

"Do you like sports?"

"I love sports. I play basketball and softball for the Catholic Youth League. And I play football with the guys in the neighborhood."

She paused and then said, "I work at the YMCA and run a youth basketball program. I could help you train for your season, and maybe you'd like to be a referee for the young kids' league?" I was thrilled at the thought of spending so much time with Liz.

As we finished our food, something occurred to her. "Have you ever had a hot fudge sundae? Not a pretend one with chocolate sauce, but one with real hot fudge?" When she discovered that I hadn't, Liz started making a list on a piece of paper she pulled from her purse. She wrote down all her ideas for things we should do: go to the movies, get involved with the YMCA sports programs, eat hot fudge sundaes, get in shape for basketball season by running together, working out at the gym, and jumping rope. "Olga, we have to do these things. All kids should have these experiences." I was thrilled, and my thoughts were intense: *I love Liz. I wish I could live with her.* I closed my fist and felt a separation inside into a part that would hold on to this experience for when I needed it.

At the end of the evening, as she was dropping me off at home, Liz asked gently, "Olga, where did you get those bruises?"

I thought for what seemed like forever but had no answer. "What bruises?"

"The ones on your back and legs that I saw this morning at the pool." Fear rose up inside me and my eyes began to flutter back and forth. Suddenly I couldn't remember what we were talking about. She pointed to the bruising on my inner thigh to illustrate her question. Horrified, I stared at it as if it were someone else's body.

I finally said, "I don't know." I felt panicky and opened the door to get out of the car but Liz stopped me.

"It's okay! It's okay. I was just wondering. Please don't go quite yet. Olga, you and I are friends, and if you ever want to talk with me about anything, you can. Okay?" I stared at her, wordless. Some parts inside me that had been having fun were worried. *What if she doesn't want to take me to Bob's Big Boy again? Will she still be my friend?* Other parts whose role it was to hide what had happened were worried for different reasons. *She's going to find out. She's going to think I'm a whore. If she finds out, I'll have to die.* But from the outside, all Liz probably saw was my dazed silence. We sat there together for a couple more minutes.

As I got out of the car, I thanked her and came back to myself a little. I asked her if we could go out again sometime. "Yes, of course," she responded quickly. "I'm sorry I made you uncomfortable. I won't ask you those questions again, but remember that you can tell me anything." I closed the car door and ran into our apartment building.

●　○　●

For the rest of that summer and for the next four years, until Alex left home to join the army, he continued his attacks on me—sometimes on his own, and sometimes with Gary or another friend. Alex raped me anywhere he felt like it: in my room, in other parts of the apartment, and in other parts of our building. He didn't seem to care if anyone saw him. He was brutal in his attacks and I fought him hard.

During one attack in my bedroom, he swung at my face with his fist but I turned away just in time. Out of the corner of my eye I saw my mom standing in the open door to my room, with a flat, distant look on her face. My heart broke. I desperately wanted her to intervene, to stop Alex. She could have. Although she had been powerless against my father, she did have power over Alex. But she had that stare in her eyes that I used to see when she tended to her roses. She hadn't seen me then, and she wouldn't see me now. My mom didn't want to face what Alex was doing to me. She turned, went into the living room, and turned on the TV. Then she turned the volume up high.

While I went on into my teen years with no specific memory of Alex's rapes, the meanness of his attacks on me left me feeling especially ugly and small. I couldn't escape the feeling that I was a bad, disgusting person. I never thought about where it came from, but I felt it all the time.

● ● ●

Around this time, my parts started taking a much more active role in my life. Rather than having the primary function of locking away memories of abuse and helping me survive attacks with the least amount of physical damage, my parts started helping me navigate my world. When Twelve formed, she was different from other parts. Because my father wasn't around to control Alex and Mike, Twelve perceived more danger and took a more active role in protecting me. She often came close to the surface and raised thoughts and feelings I didn't understand at the time. Bolstered by the presence of Twelve, the part I now think of as Eight at times came closer to my consciousness, as well, to watch and warn me about Alex and Mike. Although these parts didn't allow me access to specific memories, they would give me feelings of worry and anxiety.

I thought I was uneasy around Mike because he was so demanding and angry with my mom, always bossing her around and generally being disrespectful. Despite all this, I still had a fondness for him. Young parts remembered how fun it had been to play with Mike. He was my favorite brother, the one who taught me how to play basketball and football, the one who had said he would protect me, and I longed for the days just a few years before when I could feel his love for me.

So when Mike invited me to go with his friends to the cemetery across the street to fish in a pond one hot day that July, there was immediate conflict inside. Mike never wanted to include me in what he was doing anymore, and he spent less and less time at home. Twelve felt suspicious of his invitation, but younger parts felt special because he wanted me to come with his friends. They won the debate, and I eagerly agreed to go.

There were six of us, five boys and me, and when we got to a secluded part of the cemetery, the boys encircled me. Mike's face looked angry and bitter as he said, "You think you're better than us, bitch? Well, I know your secret, and I'm going to show them." Panic rose inside me and my thoughts flew. I didn't know it at the time, but Twelve came up to the surface quickly, with Eight just behind her. *This isn't about fishing at the pond. It's about Mike showing off for his friends.* I watched from a tree nearby as Mike and his friends took turns raping me.

This was too much for my mind to take, even from the safe distance of the tree. I loved Mike and here he was, hurting me and showing his friends how to do it too. So instead of me watching from the tree, Twelve watched as if it were happening to someone else, and I went back to the convent with the nuns and Sister Mary Joseph and Doña Graciela. Liz was there too. We all played basketball and no one got dirty or fouled out. Doña Graciela, being too old to play, led us all in the Hail Mary.

After the boys left, I waited a while before getting up. I felt lightheaded and everything was spinning. Once things inside settled down, I could barely remember what they had done and what they had said about me. Suddenly a compelling worry came up: *I could get hurt out here by myself. I have to go home right away.* I needed to get home, but I clearly looked beat up. My shirt and overalls were torn, my underwear ripped. I had to hold my clothes so they wouldn't fall off. It was a good fifteen-minute walk home, and the entire time I was consumed with worry about being seen. Many people did see me, but they tried not to make eye contact. My brother's four friends were waiting in front of our apartment building to see me come back home and find out whether it was true that I wouldn't say anything.

I felt so much humiliation when I saw them. I couldn't look at them. I dashed into the apartment without any thought of who I would run into, collected clothes to change into, and scurried to the bathroom to clean up. Another part developed to hold this humiliation. I showered for what felt like hours, staying in the warm water until the fuzziness in my head was deep enough that I couldn't feel any physical pain. I went to my room and crawled under my bed. I didn't clean the house. I didn't make dinner. My eyes began shifting back and forth uncontrollably, and soon I fell asleep.

When I didn't tell on Mike, he and his friends started seeking me out more and more. Later, I came to understand how the parts that held memories of attacks away from my subconscious and helped me survive a violent childhood worked against me as I grew up. Not having a memory of being raped left me feeling anxious and apprehensive around my brothers but unable to avoid attacks or do anything to prevent them. Although forgetting was merciful, it left me without any real protection.

That summer, Liz became like an older sister to me. We went to the movies. We ate at Bob's Big Boy. We went together to her other job at the YMCA running youth programs. She worked with me on my basketball skills and taught me how to stay in shape during the off-season. She taught me how to run long distances and how to jump rope to improve my timing, and we worked on my shooting skills. I noticed that when I was with Liz I felt safe and calm, whereas when I was at home and in my neighborhood I felt nervous. I spent as much time as I could with Liz that summer, and later, when I was old enough, I got a job so I could stay away from home even more.

6

My first month in ninth grade, I was accepted as a reporter for the high school newspaper. I really wanted to be a writer, so within the first week of school I'd asked Ms. Solinsky, my journalism teacher, about being on the newspaper staff. She was on the committee that reviewed writing samples from applicants and told me to try for it, but also warned me that freshmen were rarely accepted.

Ms. Solinsky knew my brother Alex, and I think she saw things in him that made her wonder. Alex had been a photographer on the newspaper staff for a short time, and I got a sense that Ms. Solinsky didn't get along with him. As most teachers did, the first thing she asked me when we met was "Are you related to Alex?"

"Yes, but I'm nothing like him," I said proudly. This response was usually well received, and it had the added benefit of being true. I wasn't anything like Alex and never wanted to be. Twelve, the protective part that still kept me distant from Alex, was unforgiving. I felt nothing for Alex—no empathy, no familial connection, nothing. Even though I held no memory of Alex's rapes or the rapes he encouraged his friends to commit, I was filled with suspicious thoughts about him and knew to keep my distance.

By this time, I felt that Alex had no redeeming qualities. He lied a lot. He did poorly in school, even failing some classes. He stole from my mom, from me, including the money I made babysitting, and even from school. Ms. Solinsky reluctantly reported him to the safety officer in our high school for stealing some cameras. When they called our house, he told my mom that he had bought the cameras. She didn't believe him either. He often looked like he was on drugs, staggering around unsteadily with bloodshot eyes and bumping into things.

The summer he turned sixteen, Alex was arrested for raping an eight-year-old girl in one of the storage compartments in our apartment complex's basement. Mom didn't tell me what had happened, but I heard her calling Tomás the night he was arrested. "Alex is in jail. We need money to get him out." I didn't care what happened to Alex, but I was worried about my mom, and this was one more thing for her to worry about.

Later that week I found out what had happened from a woman who lived in our building. "I'm sorry I had to call the police about your brother," she apologized. "But he was raping that poor little girl in the storage room, and it just wasn't right." I could feel my head getting fuzzy and a blank stare come up in my eyes.

Some authority, probably a judge, ordered Alex to see a therapist for a while. As far as I could tell, it didn't help.

So even though I didn't remember Alex's attacks on me, all of that gives some insight into why, when teachers asked me about him, I distanced myself as much as possible. When I told Ms. Solinsky I was nothing like him, she said, "Good!" I was surprised at how blunt and direct she was. She was stern and didn't smile or laugh very much, but she loved journalism. Anyone who worked on the newspaper staff learned quickly to respect her. In fact, sometimes Ms. Solinsky was a little scary because she raised her voice at us when she lost her patience.

She was unlike any teacher I'd had before: older, with long, wiry gray hair that she pulled back into a bun. She was also the biggest person I'd ever seen. She was tall for a woman—as tall as some of the male teachers—and very heavy. She wore big, loose-fitting, handmade dresses. Many students made fun of the fact that she had trouble walking. I didn't know what to say when people joked about her. Usually I just stayed quiet or agreed with their jokes, and then I felt bad because I knew she liked me and was watching out for me. She was behind most of my successes in high school.

I loved the other writers for the newspaper, and being one of them. They were smart and I felt smart by association, but I also always felt like I had to work harder than they did. I never told anyone at the time, but reading was very hard for me. It was hard for me to do the research necessary for the articles. I was distracted by all the thoughts in my head and couldn't seem to focus enough to understand the words. One strategy I used was reading out loud, which helped because my voice drowned out the thoughts racing through my head. I often did this in an effort to connect the words I was reading into sentences, the sentences into paragraphs, and the paragraphs into a story.

But I was terrified of people finding out I had to read out loud to understand. Most of the time no one knew because I read alone, but in journalism we were sometimes assigned reading during class time. In response, I developed a strategy of whispering the words to myself very softly. Sometimes I couldn't even hear myself, but by saying the words I could focus on them. To avoid the humiliation of being found out, I rested my hand on my chin and covered my mouth.

One day Ms. Solinsky asked me to come up to her desk during class. She quietly asked, "Are you having trouble concentrating in class? Are you having trouble reading?"

I felt exposed and ashamed. My heart fell and my chest felt tight. I know now that this sensation signals that some of my parts are close to the surface. I wondered, *How did she know? Is she like me? Does she know about me?* I felt my eyes become unfocused and got that familiar fuzzy feeling in my head but managed to answer, "Sometimes I have trouble understanding what I read. It just doesn't sink in."

Ms. Solinsky said she could tell I was trying different approaches to focus on reading. "I want to let you know how I improved my own reading comprehension in case it might work for you." Still in a daze but feeling calmer inside, I listened. "Pretend as if you're reading out loud, but don't move your lips. Just imagine that you can hear the words in your mind. This should help when you're around people. You might even decide you want to read like this all the time. It may take longer to read this way, but you'll understand what you read better and remember it longer."

I felt like Ms. Solinsky had just given me a hug. I could feel that she cared about me, and inside I felt warm and comforted. By this point I wasn't closing my fist to create positive parts of myself anymore, but as I learned to use her suggested method for reading I split off a part of myself to hold on to her kindness in teaching me how to improve my reading.

●   ●   ●

One evening in October, I left a late newspaper staff meeting to catch a bus to the YMCA, where I helped Liz with her basketball leagues every Friday night. The bus seemed particularly crowded. There were some college students, people who seemed to be on their way home from work, an old woman with groceries, another high school student, and a few men in their thirties who were dressed casually.

One of these men was wearing a ripped T-shirt and jeans and looked like he hadn't bathed in a few days. He had an unshaven face, short greasy hair, and dirty hands. The way he looked at women and girls on the bus made me nervous. He looked as if he could see through their clothes. He peered at everyone closely, as if he was looking for someone. Then he saw me and walked directly to where I was sitting.

There was no place for him to sit, so he stood in front of my seat, holding on to the passenger railing. The crotch of his pants was close to my face and I felt a little panicky inside. He inched closer, watching me closely. Conflicting thoughts raced through my mind: *Push him away! Get him away from you! Hit him! No, you can't do that or you'll get hurt really badly. Don't say anything. Get up! Get out of here! He's too close.* My head started to ache. I sat silently, turned my head away from his crotch, and stared off in an unfocused way.

"Am I standing too close to you?" came the question from above. I tried to sort out what to do, again grappling with conflicting thoughts: *He wants what the others wanted. He'll hurt you if you don't talk. Just tell him no! Don't talk to him. Yes, talk to him or he'll hurt you worse.* I couldn't hold on to any one thought and was overwhelmed. *Get away! Run! No, tell him it's okay. Don't make him mad.* I simply couldn't respond. Then he startled me by asking again.

"No," I finally answered, still staring off. He was watching me very closely and the pain in my head was getting worse. I wanted to get off the bus, but the YMCA was still far away and I worried that he might follow me.

"My name is Frank. What's your name?" *Don't say anything! Get away! Tell him or he'll hurt you.* My headache felt worse, sharper now, and I started feeling nauseous. I couldn't think. Finally, I answered, "Olga." Inside the thoughts were flying. I felt very nervous, then numb again.

"That's an unusual name. Where are you going, Olga?"

My thoughts flew and my head felt like it was filling with cotton. He asked again, this time with a firm tone. When I heard his tone, I felt like I had done something wrong.

"The YMCA." I could hear how flat I sounded.

"Where do you live?"

I acted as though I didn't hear him.

"Where do you live?" he said, again in that firm tone.

"Elmwood Apartments."

"Oh, I live right by there." I didn't respond. "Maybe I'll see you around there." I nodded, my head throbbing and my nausea getting worse. I started worrying that I was going to throw up.

My stop came and I signaled the bus to let me off. I got up and maneuvered around Frank carefully so as not to touch him. I could feel him watching me. I ran the couple of blocks to the YMCA, where Liz was waiting. She looked at me and asked, "What's going on?"

"Nothing. It's just that there was this creepy guy on the bus."

"You didn't talk to him, did you?"

I was ashamed that I had. "No, I know not to talk to strangers."

"Especially not strange men on the bus," she added. "Do you want to get changed?" I was there to officiate some basketball games for her second- and third-grade leagues. I felt better and settled down. My headache and nausea started to fade.

The games were a lot of fun. The kids were young and excited and listened well. I could blow the whistle and call an infraction, and everyone would do as I instructed. Having played basketball since I was five years old, I knew the rules really well. I had never felt so important, smart, and capable.

After the games were over, Liz and I went to Bob's Big Boy. We talked about the teams and the kids, and as always, Liz asked me how I was doing. I always said I was fine unless I was worrying about something at school. She asked about my mom and brothers. "My mom and Mike are fine and Alex is Alex." These were my standard answers. When Liz dropped me off at home, she always waited until she saw me go into my building before driving away. That night as I got out of her car, I saw a man standing in the shadows of the courtyard of our apartment building. I vaguely heard him call my name, so I turned, and then I ran into my building. I had an uneasy feeling.

The next day after school I came home on the bus. I found Alex at home in our apartment, and that made me nervous. Liz was going to pick me up on her way to work in a couple of hours, so I went outside and sat on the bench to wait. Someone came up behind me. "Olga?"

I was startled. It was creepy Frank, from the bus. He sat down and asked me why I didn't answer him the night before. I felt foggy, then numb. I shrugged. He said he had come over to see me and that I was rude for not talking to him. I went deeper inside. He asked me where I went to school, and despite the warnings I heard in my mind, I told him. "How do you get there?" he asked.

"I take the bus," I heard myself say flatly. My mind raced again with conflicting thoughts, warning me to not talk to him and telling me to run, but also warning me to not make him mad, to do what he said so I wouldn't get hurt worse. Like always, the thoughts came and went too quickly for me to examine them. I flatly answered all of his questions about what time I went to school and came home, and told him that no one was home most of the time.

What I understand now is that Frank took note of my automatic answers and dazed response to his encroachments on my personal space and privacy. It wasn't until many years later that I trained myself to respond with anger and resistance to this kind of violation. Back then, I didn't understand that my responses marked me in Frank's mind as someone he could hurt.

Frank hung around our apartment complex for several weeks. My instinct was to stay in our apartment and hide from him. But the apprehension I felt whenever Alex was home made me want to leave. I started going out the back of our building to the basketball court, but often Mike's friends—the ones who had raped me—would be there. Although I didn't remember the rape, I also didn't feel comfortable around those boys. Often I ended up wandering around the apartment complex, looking around nervously but never really knowing what I was afraid of.

Frank started driving around in his car looking for me. One late afternoon, he pulled up next to me and asked if I wanted to go to Bob's Big Boy. He had learned from our conversations that it was my favorite place to go. Despite more warnings in my mind, I got in his car. Of course, we didn't go to Bob's Big Boy. Instead, he pulled into a remote area of the cemetery and raped me. I fought back at first, but he easily overpowered me. I left my body and watched from outside the car. When he was done with me, he drove away and left me there in the dark. The parts that held deep shame came up and I was consumed by it.

● ◦ ●

The next day, Ms. Solinsky examined me carefully. "How did you get *that* bruise playing basketball?" she asked, pointing at one on my wrist. I tried hard to think clearly about what might have happened. I had noticed the bruises too, but with no real memory of the rape, I just assumed I got hurt playing sports. I smiled my perfect practiced smile and said I didn't know. She searched my face and looked at the bruises again, then asked if I had any bruises that she couldn't see. I told her I had some around my upper thighs. I was just as confused as she was, and starting to feel panicky.

Ms. Solinsky left the room and soon came back and asked me to join her in the hallway, where the school nurse was waiting. They explained that they were concerned about my injuries. The nurse asked if I would come to her office so she could examine the bruises. When I agreed, I started feeling fuzzy in my head. The nurse looked at my wrists, arms, legs, and upper thighs and a red mark on my face and asked how I possibly could have gotten all of those bruises playing basketball. I couldn't explain it and said, "I don't know. I just have the bruises and don't remember how I got them. That's the only thing I've been doing that could have caused them."

The nurse asked if she could call my mother. I agreed and then listened to her explain the situation to my mom over the phone: "It looks like she has been sexually assaulted." I could tell from the nurse's end of the conversation that my mother was saying that couldn't be true. She probably told the nurse what she always said:

"Olga is a tomboy and prone to getting bruised." The nurse hung up, frustrated.

Sexually assaulted ran through my head over and over as if it were in a foreign language. *Sexually assaulted. What does that mean?* I couldn't understand the words. I felt myself separating, my hands splitting in two. A part formed to make the words unintelligible to me, separating the words into letters and putting each letter in its own room so I couldn't put the pieces together. I sat there in a daze. The nurse asked me once again if someone had hurt me. The fogginess that filled my head was so thick that I felt like I was hearing her through a very small hole in the ground. I didn't respond.

Finally, the nurse let me know I could talk to her whenever I needed to and then took me back to journalism class. As I went back into the classroom, she pulled Ms. Solinsky into the hallway. In exhaustion, I put my head down on my desk in the back of the room and my eyes shifted from side to side until I fell asleep. I slept there the rest of the day. Later I found out that Ms. Solinsky told my other teachers that I was sick and would be in her classroom until I felt better.

When I finally woke up, school had been out for hours but Ms. Solinsky was still at her desk. "Hi there, sleepyhead," she said. I was startled, not just because it was so late, but because Ms. Solinsky was lightly trying to be funny. She drove me home that evening in her old blue Buick. She walked me up the two flights of stairs to our apartment, which I knew was hard for her, and came in with me when I unlocked the door. Knowing my mom would be mad that I brought home a visitor unannounced, I called out for her right away. She came out of the kitchen as Ms. Solinsky stood in the living room near the door. I introduced Ms. Solinsky to my mom. My mom was pleasant and asked Ms. Solinsky to please call her Blanca. She also apologized for all the trouble I had caused.

"She is no trouble at all. We're worried because she is so tired and has some bad bruises."

"Yes. I explained to the nurse who called me at work that since Olga's father died I cannot keep an eye on her as closely as I'd like," my mother said.

Ms. Solinsky replied, "I understand it must be hard to raise three children on your own, but I wanted to let you know that if I can ever help, you can call me." She put a piece of paper with her phone number on the coffee table.

"Thank you, that is very kind. I will." Of course, my mother would never call.

"It was nice to meet you, Blanca. Your daughter is a very good student, very smart. Some of the other teachers and I have become quite attached to her. We'll keep an eye on her to help make sure she has the support she needs." My mother thanked Ms. Solinsky again and closed the door behind her. As I took in Ms. Solinsky's words, I felt myself separate to hold on to what she had said about me.

I never talked to Frank after that or went anywhere with him again. He disappeared shortly afterward, but I don't know why. Meanwhile, I dissociated more and more often around people on the bus and in other crowded public places. I wish I could say Frank was the only sexual predator who recognized me as someone who was vulnerable to attack, but this sort of thing happened quite a few times during my high school years. Thankfully, Liz and some of my teachers found clubs for me to join, teams to be on, and after-school assignments to complete, so I was a little less accessible to people who could spot and take advantage of my vulnerabilities.

With the encouragement of Liz and my teachers, I excelled in sports and scholastics, speech and journalism clubs, and regional writing and speech contests. These people not only watched over me in ways I'll never fully know, but also made it possible for me to go to college. At Ms. Solinsky's instigation, several teachers submitted an application on my behalf for a full scholarship to our state university.

I was also one of three seniors, out of a class of eight hundred, chosen to address our graduating class. My mother and brothers didn't come to my graduation, but Liz took the day off to be there and sat toward the front of the family section. I talked about the hopes, dreams, and adventures our futures held, and how we had, in that moment, so much promise and potential. That fall, I began classes at our state university on a scholarship that covered my full tuition.

• ○ •

I lived at home with my mom and commuted to college. By this time, Alex had enlisted in the army and Mike was living in a dorm at his college, so home felt a little better and I was much less anxious. Because my mom had known about my brothers' attacks throughout my high school years but didn't protect me, during that time I developed parts that were resentful, angry, and hard and cold toward her. Still, I had been taught from a very young age that, as a grown woman, it would be my responsibility to care for my aging parents, and it was clear that my mom still expected me to do this. As a result, I went back and forth between feeling nothing for my mom to being cold and angry to being drawn to taking care of her. I avoided being at home and kept busy with two part-time jobs.

My first day on campus, registration day, the crowds and chaos overwhelmed me. I walked into an enormous building full of long lines of students, all of them talking and laughing with an anxious excitement that you could cut with a knife. The system of signing up for classes made no sense to me. My thoughts raced, leaving me confused and disoriented. Then I felt calm and numb, but that didn't help me accomplish what I needed to get done. My head filled with cotton and I felt paralyzed, unable to either think clearly or talk.

Then I heard a familiar voice. It was Liz, who was on campus because she had returned to school to get another degree. She took my arm and we stood together in line. My sense of disconnection eased a bit. As the numbness slowly receded, I felt so much gratitude for Liz's friendship and so much love for her. I wasn't alone.

The woman behind the registration table explained to us that one of my required classes, in the English Department, was full; I had to find the professor and get her approval for an extra student in her class. Overwhelmed, I said, "Forget it. This is just too hard. I don't know where any of the buildings are." I felt defeated. "Maybe this was a mistake."

"This happens all the time," Liz said, and the woman behind the table agreed. "I'll go with you. It will be fine. You'll see." Liz registered for her own classes quickly, thanked the woman for her help, and said, "Let's go." My thoughts had calmed and I felt more connected to my surroundings, but I was exhausted from all the activity in my head. Liz showed me the campus on the way to the English Department, and when we got there the professor signed the form letting me into her class. I was all set.

• • •

Mike visited home often that year. One night early in the first semester, I was surprised to see him drop by with his friend Harold. Normally he didn't want his friends to meet us or see our home, but he explained to Mom that they were hungry. She quickly made them Dominican black beans and white rice, with a flank steak seasoned with garlic and onions. It was a traditional meal for us, but for some reason I wanted no part of it. That night as Mike and Harold settled in for a visit, I went into my room to study. But not even reading out loud penetrated the fog in my head, so I decided to shower and get ready for bed. I closed the bathroom door, undressed, and got into the shower, still fighting a heavy sense of dread and anxiety.

The bathroom door opened and Mike burst in. I yelled at him to get out, but he wouldn't. Mike gestured for Harold to join us in the bathroom. I instantly panicked and then left my body. In the background, I heard my mom turn up the volume on the TV. They raped me in the shower that night. When they were done, they dried off, got dressed, and left. I heard them thanking my mom for dinner, and my mom responding that it had been nice to meet Harold.

I stood in the bathroom, cold and shivering. *I need to shower,* I thought over and over. Even though I had just gotten out of the shower, the thought kept coming. I sat there naked until there was more hot water. As I showered again, I split off into a number of parts I think of as Eighteen, who held the memory of this attack. Afterward, I dried off. Still in a daze, I opened the medicine cabinet and found a bottle of pills, some sort of over-the-counter pain reliever, and as I held the bottle in my hand I felt my hand separate into two. At that moment another part formed, almost like an entry area, to separate me from all of the eighteen-year-old parts. This part would take action to keep me from knowing how horrible my life was and how alone I was. *I will never be safe* ran through my mind repeatedly. In this entry area, as in many other rooms, were plans and the intention to kill myself. This part held my sense that my despair would be endless and inescapable, and suicide seemed the only option. I took all of the pills in the bottle, hoping there would be enough.

But once this part had done its job and its door had shut again, I no longer remembered taking the pills. I felt hard and uncaring, a new protective shell forming to keep me from ever again thinking that Mike would protect me or care about me. I simply didn't care about him anymore. I got dressed for bed and went to sleep, then woke up in the middle of the night and threw up, thinking, *I must have the flu. I haven't eaten anything weird.* Then a different thought came: *Just die.*

The next morning I got up with no memory of either being attacked or taking the pills. Instead, I worried about my classes and my friendship with Liz as I got dressed and left for school.

I eventually found even more ways to avoid being at home, including studying with friends. Liz happily spent entire nights in the library with me, studying and taking naps. Other friends let me stay in their dorm rooms when I said I was too tired to make it home at night.

• • •

College was a big challenge to my reading skills. Each class had several books as required reading, difficult books written by big thinkers. When I could, I read out loud, and when I was around others I read out loud in my head, as Ms. Solinsky had taught me to do. Either way, it was very slow. I felt discouraged by all the work and how challenging it was. Inside, I was in constant struggle with self-doubt, wondering, *Why did I think I could make it through college? I can't even read.* I looked around in the library, saw all the smart students, and felt sure I didn't belong there. *I'm stupid. I can't do this. I'm wasting the state's money.* The thoughts came faster and stronger. I felt a catch in my chest and my head spun. I felt like I was going to jump out of my skin. Dully, I stared at my reading assignments.

I noticed Liz, who studied with me in the library most nights, watching me from across the table. Deep inside, I was comforted by her presence and put my head down on the desk to take a break from all the thoughts. Liz came over to me and quietly asked what was wrong. I concentrated hard and tried to turn the thoughts in my head into words. Finally I responded, "I can't do this. I can't understand what I'm reading. I'm just stupid."

Liz was surprised. She had never heard me worry about my schoolwork and knew I had done well in high school. "College is different, Olga. They give you a lot more to read. But you can do this. I know you are smart enough." I pushed through the fog and raised my head. "You just have to find your way." I let the words linger in my head: *I just have to find my way.* After a few moments, Liz added,

"When we're done, I know an all-night diner where we can get something to eat." The excitement at the thought of this ran through me. I was soothed by her encouraging words and delighted at the thought of pie or ice cream at the end of all this hard work.

For the next few weeks, I kept Liz's words with me in philosophy class. To compensate for my difficulty with reading, I focused a lot more on what the professor said. My mind had created a part that would learn by listening, watching, and discussing. When I didn't understand a point, I went to my professor's office to clarify what was meant. During exams, I found myself able to remember the exact day when we talked about particular points in class. When I focused hard during a lecture, I could later hear the discussion in my mind as if watching a movie clip and could visualize the words on the chalkboard. I thought this was something everyone could do.

Ironically, I made it through high school and college largely thanks to my good memory. I believe that my ability to replay discussions or visualize notes on a chalkboard at exam time arose from all those years of instinctively capturing images and sounds of attacks in my mind. Although the memories of the abuse were stored in rooms that were locked and inaccessible to me, the instinctive capturing of pictures and movies in my head had become a skill of sorts and worked to my advantage even in settings that weren't traumatic. I developed the habit of focusing intently on lessons, lectures, and discussions and unintentionally honed my memory skills even further.

Of course, good recall didn't help me if I didn't pay close attention in class or simply didn't attend class at all. The state university I attended was so large that it was overwhelming and often hard for me to navigate. I felt anxious walking across campus from the parking area to my classes, and once I got to my classrooms, they were usually crowded. So I often skipped class, and after the first two years of college I had a 2.5 GPA to show for it. Liz was surprised at my low grades. So, with her encouragement, I resolved to try harder. In my junior and senior years I went to every class and sat up front so I could be sure to focus. In this way, I eventually raised my GPA to about 3.5 and earned a bachelor's degree in political science.

• • •

I still avoided being at home even though Alex and Mike rarely dropped by anymore. My mom worked all day, saw Tomás on Saturdays, and was alone most evenings. Because she didn't have any real friends, she turned to me. However, after wanting my mom's attention for so many years, I no longer needed it when it was finally available. In fact, by this time I was mostly hard and protected in regard to my mother. But when I saw her sad, lonely, or scared, the parts inside of me whose job it was to protect her from my father came forward; the doors to those rooms opened, and I took care of her. She could almost always draw those parts out.

When I was home studying, she often wanted me to watch TV with her or take her to the grocery store. She wanted me to go to the movies with her, but not fun movies like *Aliens*, which I watched with Liz. My mom preferred movies that I didn't enjoy, like *Dr. Zhivago*. She wanted to go out to eat with me and Liz and wanted me to invite my friends over. I resisted her suggestions and felt increasingly resentful and bitter.

I lived with my mom all through college and for a year after that while I worked full-time. But after working for my local senator, I decided that what I really wanted to do was enter politics, and to do so, I had to study law. I was accepted into George Washington University in D.C., and soon afterward broke the news to my mom that I was moving. It was hard. I have always loved her so much, and there were parts that still very much wanted to stay with her and take care of her. Mom cried, then felt abandoned and angry, and then became indifferent.

After I told her, I had difficulty thinking anytime I was around her, my head fuzzy and foggy. I thought about her all the time. I now know that parts that were resentful, cold, and self-protective were in conflict with parts that wanted to take care of her. I had to work very hard to keep my resolve to leave. So many times I heard in my head, "Mom, I'm sorry. I'll stay." But I didn't say it.

My first year of law school I worked full-time for a senator, part-time at a pharmacy, and part-time for a labor lawyer, and went to school at night. I studied late at night and on the weekends. I didn't get much sleep. The classes were scary and huge, with lots of students. During the first few classes, each teacher sent around a seating chart and had us write our names in the boxes corresponding to our chair locations. "This will be your permanent seat for this class," belted out one professor. "Make sure you like it, because you won't be moving." I moved up front as soon as I heard that, knowing I would get distracted if I sat too far back. The seating chart helped each professor call on individual students to ask questions about the cases we were assigned to read each night. You never knew when you would be called on in front of a hundred students, and some professors made the experience very embarrassing.

This was hard for most new students, and particularly hard for me because I was terrified of unpredictability, especially if it brought with it the possibility of being humiliated. As a professor explained the process to us that first day, my mind raced with fears: *He's going to hurt you in front of all these people. We have to get out of here!* came a scream from within. *You just aren't smart enough for this. What made you think you could do this?* For years now, I'd sometimes had this sense of several parts within me speaking as one, and it felt natural to me. The self-doubt brought on panic, then a calm fuzziness settled over me.

Despite these early challenges, I felt better than I could ever remember feeling. I felt much calmer than when I lived with my mom. Even though we still spoke on the phone every day, I didn't have to be afraid of the hurt that I had always experienced around her. So despite my hectic schedule, I felt much more relaxed. My head didn't get that fuzzy feeling as often.

But at night I often woke up in a sweat, confused by all sorts of weird dreams—strangely vivid dreams about having sex with men, some I knew and some I didn't. As far as I knew, I was a virgin. I hadn't even really dated in high school or college. I'd think about that and wonder why I had those sexual dreams over and over again, and then I'd be overtaken by worry about law school and finances— my new obsessions. My old coping strategies were still there in full force: I worried about not being smart enough. I worried that my professors would decide I had only mistakenly been admitted to law school. I worried about failing, about not having enough money, about having to quit school and move back home with my mom. I had taken out large student loans to make ends meet, and I worried about owing so much money.

There was also a deeper level of worry going on, a series of con-nected racing thoughts that I could sometimes hear: *I don't know where I'm going. I've never been here before. It's not safe to go to new places. I could get hurt. On the subway, someone could be waiting to attack me.* In the past I couldn't catch these thoughts long enough to ponder them, but now, every so often I could. Still, I was practiced at avoiding thoughts. I would catch one of these deeper worries and wonder about it briefly, and then off my mind would go into another worry about school or finances.

●　●　●

In the first week of classes, I was looking for the classroom for Contracts 101. The hallway at the Law Center was narrow, and I got caught up in the bustle of students coming and going. Halfway down and to the right was an open area, a student lounge where some students were waiting for evening classes to start. The short walk through the crowded hallway left me feeling panicky and overwhelmed, but the feel of the students in the lounge was different. They seemed friendlier, so I gravitated toward the open area.

I worked up the focus and courage to ask a couple of guys sitting at a table if they knew where Contracts 101 was being held. One of them had dark hair and eyes and a kind smile. He told me, "It's down the hall. But you can't go in yet because the class in there hasn't ended." Then he reached out his hand and introduced himself. "Hi, I'm Raymond, and this is David," he said, pointing to the guy sitting next to him. David looked up and I could tell he was shy. He had dark brown hair, a receding hairline, the bluest eyes I had ever seen, and a wide smile. It turned out that Raymond and David were in Contracts 101 too. I had no idea that I had just met the man I would marry—the man who would teach me how to study and the kindest man I would ever know.

While we waited together for the classroom to open up that first day, we chatted. "Night school makes sense to me," Raymond said, "because in the day program the competition is tougher. Night school students all have jobs, so your odds of doing well in comparison are better. I thought I'd start here, get in the top 10 percent, do law review, and switch to the day program." I was filled with self-doubt and my thoughts started racing: *I have to work three jobs. I'm never going to be able to compete with people like Raymond. Who do I think I am? Who do I think I'm fooling?* On the outside I probably looked distracted, a bit in a daze. Inside, I was struggling to focus.

David's voice came gently: "How did you end up at GW's night program?" I looked up at him and instantly got lost in his bright blue eyes.

"I want to go into politics, and everyone I know in politics has a law degree. This was the best law school I got into." David looked at me intently, listening to every word. He seemed genuinely interested in what I had to say.

"How about you?" I asked him.

"I grew up on a farm, and my father wanted me to do something better than he did. I studied chemical engineering and worked for a couple years as an engineer. But I hated the work, so I saved up to go to law school. I applied to some schools in New York, but D.C. seems the place to be to be an environmental lawyer." I hung on every word. David was so thoughtful. He had it all planned out. He seemed to have so much energy and enthusiasm. He was full of hope and anticipation of things to come.

Soon the classroom opened up, and we all walked in together. I followed David and Raymond down the long steps of the large lecture hall. I wanted to sit with them, but four of their friends had shown up, and I didn't want to seem pushy and invite myself into the group. So I followed the six of them, and when they went into the second row from the front, I went into the row behind them and sat right behind David and Raymond. I could easily have become overwhelmed in that large classroom full of noisy students. But I'd felt safe in the short time I'd talked with David and Raymond and thought, *I'll just stay with them.* I sat with them in class that first day, and in subsequent classes for years to come.

Law school challenged me more than any previous educational experience. Before, my success was in large part due to being able to recall specific words on a page or a chalkboard or remembering snippets from a lecture. Law was a completely new language, and I didn't understand it. The lectures didn't always offer what I needed to do well on exams, and we only took one exam in most classes—one exam that the entire semester's grade was based on. I had to work hard to adapt to learning in this environment.

In that first week, I was sure I was in over my head. I couldn't keep up with the reading, and even when I was able to read, I couldn't understand many of the words. I hadn't bought a law dictionary yet because they were expensive, so I used the copy at the library or tried to figure out the meaning of the words from the context of the sentences. That was a big mistake. I got really behind, and the workload felt impossible. In Contracts 101 alone, we were assigned one hundred pages of reading per class, and we met three nights a week.

A month into the semester, Raymond asked me if I wanted to come over and study with him and David. I agreed, but inside I was unsure: *I'm so far behind. What if they find out I have no idea what I'm doing? They won't like me when they find out I'm stupid.* As we sat there with our books open, I noticed that they weren't relying on the textbooks as much as they were on other books—things called "outlines" and "nutshells." As we talked about the cases, I tried to write everything down but couldn't keep up with the discussion. I felt more and more stupid and wanted to cry. Finally, I blurted out, "How do you two know all this already?"

David reminded me that they were able to study during the day while I was working, but then he pulled out his outlines and nutshells. "These will tell you what's important about the case. Then if you don't have time to read the whole case, it's okay."

I was so relieved. "Where do I get those?"

David told me the name of the bookstore that carried them at the best price and offered to take me there. That weekend we went to the bookstore and afterward went back to their place to study and make pizza. Raymond didn't mind paying for delivery, but David was watching his savings and I didn't have any money, so we made pizza from scratch, which was a new experience for me. That weekend I also learned how to use an index, a table of contents, and the *Black's Law Dictionary* that I'd bought.

My mind instinctively developed new parts to specialize in the skills I needed to make it through law school. They learned to focus on the important information: the outlines, the nutshells, and what each case meant. That first year, though, while David and Raymond finished in the top 10 percent, I finished in the bottom 10 percent. Raymond was with me the day I got a D in Civil Procedure. I was so ashamed. My thoughts raced, full of humiliation, and I voiced them out loud: "I don't belong here. I should quit now before I lose any more money."

Raymond was surprised and said, "Look, you had one bad class. You did well in your other classes. You're getting the hang of this and you'll be a good lawyer. All this means is that you won't work at one of the big law firms."

I don't know why, but I believed him. Raymond, David, and I talked about it and came up with a plan: I would get a new, better-paying job so I could quit my part-time jobs, and I would move closer to school so I didn't waste so much time going back and forth. The plan worked. I spent all my free time studying with Raymond and David at their house or at the library. We often met in a big study group with some of the smartest students in our class. The conversations we had during those study sessions stuck in my mind, and I could recall them easily during exams. That year I got straight As. The three of us celebrated together, and Raymond reminded me of the day I wanted to quit. I was the safest I had ever been. I was further from my family than I'd ever been. I was happy.

7

Once I got the hang of law school, I did very well. David and I studied together more and more often and became best friends. In my third year, David and I moved in together, and the fourth year we married. Our classmates couldn't believe that we were willing to miss two weeks of the semester to go on our honeymoon, but we both already had jobs lined up and didn't feel the pressure that many of the other students felt. I eventually graduated in the top 30 percent of my class, and David was in the top 15 percent. We had both gotten jobs at big law firms, making more money than people our age should.

I had never known what it felt like to be loved so well. David cared about what I thought, what I liked, and what I didn't like. He did things I liked to do just so we could spend more time together. He had never been a runner or even a morning person before he met me, but he often got up at 5:30 a.m. to run with me. He hadn't been much of a football or basketball fan either, but after we married he would sit with me all Sunday afternoon in the fall watching football teams he didn't really care about. And during March Madness he would pull out the schedule in the paper and fill out his picks. We'd hang on every close game.

As I watched David enjoy himself doing things I cared about, I felt so good inside—almost a feeling of joy. At the time I didn't know why it was so compelling. But now I know that all the parts that I instinctively created to function well in my day-to-day life felt good to be the center of his attention. We all got to do things with him. I often thought, *I am so lucky to have found someone who wants to be with me so much. I'm not alone anymore.*

I did the same for David, cultivating an interest in things he enjoyed. He loved playing chess and wanted me to play with him. He always won, but I often came close. This also filled me with positive thoughts: *David wants me to play with him. He has lots of friends that he could visit and hang out with. He wants me.* When he wanted to start playing golf, I was right there with him, and inside I was thrilled. Every Sunday morning, bright and early after our daily run, we were at the driving range or the golf course. We often used it as an excuse to get together with friends from law school.

Still, there were wrinkles in my newfound happiness, things I struggled with for reasons I couldn't explain. Controlling my environment was still a compelling need for me. I did everything I could to not be surprised by anything. When I'd lived with roommates, I always tried to nail down plans and predict any possible changes to those plans in an attempt to have control over my life. It had been hard. I wasn't very flexible and my roommates' lives had been unpredictable. With David I felt safer than I ever had. But now that I wasn't single anymore, my life felt less predictable and less within my control. Looking back, I think that my need to predict how my day was going to unfold was a direct response to the amount of chaos in my childhood. When something changed regarding plans David and I had made, I got angry with him.

For example, I wanted to run the same path every day. I had a routine around running, and I wanted David to follow my routine. I didn't know this consciously; it was just the way my parts managed my world to try to keep me safe. One day David said he was tired of our path and wanted to run a different route. I resisted the change but couldn't explain why. We argued, but David eventually agreed that we could run the new path another day. Another time, David decided to speed up and run ahead. I felt threatened inside in a way I couldn't explain. I tried to keep up, but I wasn't as strong or as fast as David. The sudden change frightened me, and I had trouble catching my breath. I didn't know then that I was afraid because things had changed suddenly—a situation that matched the unpredictability of my childhood. I simply thought I was out of shape. When I was finally able to catch up with David, I was very angry. "Why are you running ahead? You are either going to run with me, or you're going to run ahead. I just need to know. I can't settle into my run otherwise!"

David's stunned expression made me feel ashamed. I loved him and I could see I'd hurt him. I didn't understand it back then, but the parts I had created throughout my life were becoming more active than they'd ever been. Internal conversations happened more and more. But rather than speeding through my mind so fast I couldn't catch them, the thoughts came more slowly, at a pace at which I could ponder them. They felt like conflicting thoughts, but stronger and more compelling: *Doesn't David know I have to do it the same way every time? Why am I yelling at him? He's bored with this run. He can run faster than I can. What's wrong with that? His feelings are hurt.* I suddenly apologized for yelling at him and for being mad. I felt stupid and small for being so inflexible. I heard Mike's voice in my head: "You are such a bitch. Can't you just chill out and let us have fun?"

David and I worked around my controlling behavior without ever really naming it or discussing it. My indirect and sometimes manipulative ways of communicating, my need for control over my environment, and my need to know what to expect felt completely natural and justified. Despite all of this, our life was full of fun and adventure. And for the most part, it was orderly, controlled, and predictable. Although that may not sound very romantic, it was wonderful for me. I needed stability.

David was supportive in other ways, as well. He helped me get through my challenges at work. Sometimes I still had difficulty reading and focusing, and looking back on it I realize that this usually happened when I was triggered by a situation that somehow resembled a setting in which I was abused. The perceived threat could be a place, a person, a smell, or an event and might appear entirely benign to others. These situations came up quite a bit in the environment of a large law firm. The partners, who were mostly men, gave me assignments I had to accomplish to succeed in the firm. There was a pervasive feeling among the staff that if you weren't smart enough or fast enough, you would be fired. I always felt insecure and vulnerable there. In some ways, it matched the times that my parents prostituted me. Money came with performance.

When one of the partners gave me a research assignment, I often went to the law library at David's firm, which was only a block away. I would complete the assignment there, with David helping me as he did his own work. David didn't see himself as particularly kind and generous, but I saw those traits in him every day. My time with him was magical. I felt his love for me constantly. I was the center of his world, and everything else—work, friends, family—came next. I loved it, but I didn't trust it. All of the parts that had developed to keep me distant and safe didn't know how to let me be close to someone and vulnerable.

Even though, intellectually, I never thought David would stop loving me this way, I was always worried about losing him. In general, I worried that people could look inside me, past my practiced smile, and see the fraud I felt I was. I myself didn't even know what was inside of me, but I could sense an inner heaviness, and I feared it would overtake me and destroy the life I'd built for myself—a life of happiness and success.

Ignorant of all the memories stored away in the heavily guarded rooms within me, I believed that I had overcome a childhood of poverty to get through college, become a lawyer, and have a happy marriage. I had very little memory of my childhood. I knew that we had been poor. I remembered my father as strict, and that he died when I was eleven years old. I tried not to think about growing up and kept my childhood very separate from who I had become.

After about two years, David and I both left the large law firms we had joined after law school and went to work for the federal government. My work at the Department of Justice was predictable and secure, yet interesting.

David taught me the value of saving money. I knew that I should save money to help my family, but I didn't understand saving as a long-term goal because it wasn't something that had ever happened in my family. Of course, when I was growing up it was hard to save because we were poor, but whenever my mom did get a little extra money she spent it impulsively on extravagant things.

I liked that David and I thought through our purchases carefully, but I often wanted to buy things that David thought we didn't need. For example, David couldn't imagine having to replace his record collection with CDs. The new technology was out and widely used for years before we bought a CD player or any CDs. We didn't own a computer until well after everyone we knew had one. David's thriftiness became something I and our friends gently teased him about. But as hard as it was at times, David taught me that we could save and wait, and still have things we wanted. It was his philosophy that if something worked, we didn't need to replace it. This approach allowed us to pay off our student loans in five years and buy a townhouse in a nice neighborhood. Later, it allowed me to pay for the kind of care I needed when my memories finally surfaced and my parts started coming forward.

It was a sharp learning curve for me—and for my entire family. My mother was now earning a good salary and didn't have anyone else to provide for. My brothers had also worked hard to get jobs that paid well. Now middle class, they bought whatever they wanted without much thought as to whether they could afford it. My mom accumulated all sorts of kitchen gadgets and expensive appliances even though she didn't like to cook, and even though her mounting debt overwhelmed her. Mike bought expensive clothes and went on extravagant vacations. At the age of twenty-nine, unmarried and living alone, he had a huge house and three cars, one a BMW. He lived in debt, and when the market took a downward turn, he lost the house and his cars.

We had never taken vacations when I was little, but David and I went on one or two frugal trips each year. Even though I appreciated frugal vacationing in principle, it was a challenge for me. The hotels David found were always basic, and in some cases not very clean. I didn't know then why they bothered me so much, but I was afraid to go into the rooms. All I knew at the time was that a hotel reminded me of a house that I had visited or lived in when I was little.

The first time this happened had been on our honeymoon, which we spent in Spain. When we arrived in Madrid after spending a week on the beaches of Majorca, David was worried about money. Majorca had been much more expensive than we had expected. So at the airport, David proposed that we take a bus to our hotel. Because I get sick on buses, I wanted to take a cab. We debated the issue for a little while and I pretended to concede. Since David didn't speak Spanish, he was at my mercy. I asked the information desk where I could get a cab and told David that there were no buses. He could tell that I had lied to him because we saw bus after bus go by while we were waiting in line for a cab. When I finally got in a cab, I gave the driver the address of our hotel. David reluctantly joined me and off we went.

Twenty dollars later, we pulled up at our "hotel"—a dirty, run-down hostel with about fifty high-school-aged boys waiting to check in. I looked at David in horror and told him that I couldn't stay there. He agreed but refused to pay for another cab, so we walked through the streets of Madrid, dragging our luggage behind us, looking for another place to stay. Every hotel we found was completely booked, but at each I was told that a hotel called the Reina would have a vacancy.

I finally called the Reina from a pay phone to book a room for the rest of our stay. David asked me to find out how much the rooms cost. When they said $160 per night, I knew David wouldn't agree to stay there, so I refused to tell him. He reluctantly joined me in another cab, and another twenty dollars later, we pulled up in front of a five-star hotel. David was furious.

At the front desk, I pulled out my credit card and paid for a week. David saw the statement and, furious all over again, insisted, "We are not staying here!" I told him it was too late, I had just paid. When the bellman came to help us with our bags, David declined even though he was exhausted. "I'm not paying a bellman to carry my bags fifty feet to my room when I've been hauling them all over Madrid." We rode up the elevator in silence.

Back home, we told this story as a funny example of David's thriftiness. Now I see it as an example of how deeply threatened I was by the lack of control and unpredictability that come with traveling. A strange city, buses filled with strangers, crowds of teenage boys, dirty hostels, worries about money, conflict with David when he was the only person I knew there—all of these elements threatened my sense of safety. Intellectually, I knew that I was behaving inflexibly and even manipulatively, but I was too overwhelmed to help it.

As I was growing up, no one in my family got their needs met through respectful negotiation and compromise. The only victories I had ever seen my mom achieve were small, and she had accomplished them through manipulation, which was one of the few techniques she had for surviving her relationship with my father. Later, after his death, manipulation had become a way of life for her. It became innate for me too, even though I wanted her to be more direct, and I hated it when she manipulated me.

●　○　●

Up to this point, five years into my marriage, I had been managing my everyday life through a series of parts: parts that worked, parts that ran and worked out, parts that went on vacation, and parts that went to dinner parties and were extroverted. Some parts experienced my sexual relationship with David.

Although David and I thought we had a good relationship, our intimate relationship, both emotional and sexual, was a big challenge. We didn't know why, but there were a few clues—and I did my best to avoid them. In my conscious mind, David was the only man I'd had sex with, besides someone I briefly dated early in law school. The first time we had sex was physically painful and confusing for me, and I think my response hurt David's confidence. I wasn't scared of him in any way, but my response to any sexual contact was to feel fuzziness in my head, then leave myself cognitively and perform the act without any desire or passion. What David saw was that I was in a daze and not particularly participatory. He concluded that I wasn't into the sex and felt it was his fault. He tried to make it more exciting for me, but I remained detached and quiet and mostly lay still or went through the motions.

David was tender and caring. He never wanted to do anything that felt uncomfortable or hurt, sexually or in any other regard. We were both operating under the assumption that I had very little experience, so he always checked before he did anything. I loved this about him. I didn't know how important it was to me until much later. It made me feel so safe with him. But no matter how gentle and considerate he was as a lover, being intimate was always a trigger, bringing up the abuse I'd experienced. At first I would feel a quick panic, then I felt fuzziness in my head and left my body.

Early in the first year in our marriage, David sat me down and asked me if I was sure I really loved him. Was I attracted to him? Was he doing something wrong? The pain on his face broke my heart. I loved David as much as I could love anyone; I just wasn't interested in having sex with him—or anyone else for that matter.

Still, I wanted the relationship to succeed. We both did. We worked hard at making this part of our relationship as good as the other parts. We read couples self-help books. We saw a therapist who told me I had to have sex with David if I wanted our marriage to work. She told me to fantasize or read erotica.

The truth is, with the parts inside me working hard to just get me through my days, I had a very limited range of feeling. That was the point, of course. Parts that held feelings about the violence I had endured kept those emotions away from me. Protective parts that had developed long ago helped me not feel love for those closest to me so I wouldn't feel the pain of their betrayals. This kind of distance was all I knew, and now that I was with someone I loved and could trust, the protective parts wouldn't let me feel it. I often tried to break through those parts. Focusing on David, I would look at his eyes, his smile, and his small frame and think about everything he did for me and had done for me, and I would feel how much I loved him. Feeling that much love for him felt so good, but distance was my way of being, and it always returned.

Often David felt my distance as indifference. I think he experienced me as an anxious and sometimes moody person, but loved me nonetheless. Unfortunately, as much as I wanted to change, I had no idea how to go about it. David's unwavering devotion to me was what kept us together for so long—that and the fact that even though our emotional and physical intimacy was limited, David and I continued to have fun. We vacationed, we played, we laughed. I felt safe with him. I believe that David never would have left me. I felt his adoring love and respect, and it humbled me. I was grateful for it, but I never felt I deserved it.

David and I bought a townhouse in an orderly neighborhood. Every day on our way to work, we held hands as we walked to the subway station together. We sat together, David reading the paper while I listened to music on my Walkman. Our offices were only blocks apart, so we got off at the same stop, walked as far as we could together, and then kissed and wished each other a good day. At the end of each day, David called me to see how much longer I needed to work. He would work just as long so we could walk back to the subway and ride home together.

●　○　●

I did well at the Department of Justice. Some of my parts were very hard workers. My well-developed memory helped me remember people: their names and positions and what they said during meetings. Rather than making me seem checked out, my dissociation made me seem calm and collected. In fact, the general dissociative state I was always in helped me function very well. I collected information, interacted on a personal and professional level, and was quite adept at managing most tasks in my life from this superficially numb and calm place. Most people, including me, didn't notice. This way of being and interacting was really all I knew.

From that mild dissociation, I quickly went into a deeper dissociative state if there was conflict around me, if someone expressed strong emotions, or if something unpredictable happened. Although these difficult situations triggered me, they brought out behavior that helped me do well when the going got tough. I loved solving problems and getting into the thick of things and also had well-developed skills in reading people and anticipating their needs. All of this helped me stand out, and I rose through the ranks quickly. By the age of thirty, I was the highest-ranking lawyer at the Office of Justice Programs. David, who had helped me get through law school, was proud of me. I was proud of myself too.

●　○　●

Neither my mom nor my brother Mike cared about or tried to understand the significance of my rise at the Department of Justice, but I wasn't surprised or disappointed. My marriage to David had changed my relationship with my family in many ways. When David and I went to visit my mom, she treated me well and seemed interested in our lives, focusing less on what she needed from me or how I should be taking care of her.

Mom saved those conversations for our daily phone calls because she thought David wouldn't find out about this other side of her. But he could see the changes in me when I talked to my mom. And when we made a down payment on a car and a condominium for my mother, David didn't like it, but he supported my decision anyway. It upset him to see my family spend so much money and watch me rescue them. He didn't like bailing my mom out of the consequences of her impulsive buying decisions and encouraged me to help her set up a budget instead. Eventually we agreed that I would pay off her outstanding debt, help her set up a budget, and then quit providing her with money.

David encouraged me not to talk to my mom so much because it left me feeling bad about myself. He had a weird feeling about my family and noticed the lack of boundaries, respect, and kindness. Mike spoke badly of Alex behind his back, and my mom complained about Mike in the same way, but no one ever talked directly about these things. David didn't like the way my brother Mike talked to my mom and me. Mike often tried to talk to David, man to man, about a woman's role in the home, and David openly disagreed with him. I think Mike sensed David's disapproval and kept a distance. That was helpful for me. I stopped compulsively doing things for them as best I could.

• • •

A year or so into our marriage, I started mentioning to David that I thought I might be different from other people. "Do your legs hurt?" I asked one day.

He looked puzzled. "No, why would they?"

"Mine ache all the time." I said. My body hurt all over every day, especially my joints. David and I thought it might be arthritis.

Sometimes I got fleeting but sharp vaginal or anal pain, but I didn't ask him about that.

I finally decided to consult a rheumatologist about the chronic pain. He diagnosed me with fibromyalgia and explained that it was a sleep disorder. "The pain is caused when you don't get deep enough sleep to allow your muscles to restore themselves."

I didn't understand how this could be true and said, "I'm sleeping as well as I always have." For some reason, I didn't connect my nightmares and night sweats to the issue of how well I slept.

"You told me that you've always had this pain. Is it possible that there were stressors when you were young that disrupted your sleep?"

"I was always anxious about school and sports. Otherwise, what I remember about my childhood was good." I was confused and thought, *I've always slept well.* I tried to think about what might be responsible for any sleep difficulties, but my mind felt slow and thick, and suddenly I felt very tired. "What do I do about the pain now?"

"Well, we need to ensure you get good, deep sleep. Exercise helps. Yoga and meditation will also help—and a good diet."

I heard this as if the doctor were at other end of a long tunnel. I had trouble connecting his words into sentences with meaning. I thought, *I'm in great shape*, and, speaking slowly, said, "I run every day and lift weights. Why isn't that helping?"

"Are you okay?" the doctor asked.

His question startled me and I looked at him. "I'm fine."

He looked at me carefully. "You have a stare in your eyes. Have you had this before?"

I thought about it. "Other doctors have noticed the stare, too. They've tested me for thyroid problems. It always comes back negative. Do you think it has anything to do with my pain?"

"It's possible. Sometimes a stare comes from too much anxiety or stress. Your system can become overwhelmed." I didn't know it then, but parts inside were scared because he was looking at us so closely. *He's getting too close. He's going to find out about us.* I didn't make the effort to try to catch any of these thoughts. "It could be anxiety," he continued. "Maybe from work? Being a lawyer can be stressful. Or it could also be something from the past." I felt a catch in my chest and a pulsing in my ears and then I felt calm and numb, with a fuzziness that I couldn't think through, much thicker than before. He watched me for a few seconds and then said, "There are medications that may help, but you really should try to figure out why you aren't sleeping well." He prescribed a muscle relaxant and a small dose of an antidepressant, and I started taking them each evening. I also took ibuprofen three times a day to take the edge off the pain. Right away, I noticed a difference in how deeply I slept, and eventually I got relief from most of the chronic pain.

For the next several weeks, I thought about my conversation with the doctor. It finally occurred to me that not everyone had night sweats and strange dreams. I asked David about it. He was concerned. I also told him that sometimes when I looked in the mirror, I didn't see who I thought I should see. "Sometimes I look older than I feel. Sometimes my hands seem bigger than they should be or I feel taller than I think I should be." At other times, seemingly out of nowhere, I started thinking in Spanish, which was especially strange because I hadn't spoken Spanish regularly since my father died and we could speak English at home.

As my trust in David and my love for him grew, I felt safer, so I could afford to pay attention to things I'd had to ignore or avoid before. With my newfound sense of safety came strange thoughts and fragments of scenes flashing in my head. They came slowly enough for me to see them clearly, but out of context, and I didn't understand what they meant. More and more often, I woke up drenched in sweat. Cold and damp, I would mechanically get up, change my pajamas, and go back to sleep. In my dreams, people broke into our house to kill David and hurt me. Or I'd be in a strange place, and even though no one else was there, I knew I was there to be hurt. Sometimes I dreamed in Spanish. In these dreams I was often under my bed praying and people were trying to break in. While I could remember the dreams in the morning and wondered about them, I didn't ponder them for very long. Instead, my old coping skills would intervene and I'd carry on with my life, fretting over paying bills or making a presentation at work.

This continued for several years—until the day David and I went to the movie *Thelma and Louise*. At the beginning of the movie, one of the main characters is almost raped in a vividly detailed scene. As I watched, I started having trouble catching my breath and my head started spinning. Looking back, I understand that this was caused by parts running to warn me or distract me, or with hopes of finally being known. My abdomen hurt terribly, and I was scared. Nothing like this had ever happened to me before. The pain got worse and my panic grew. I felt like I was going to jump out of my skin. The thoughts racing through my head were in both English and Spanish.

I had to leave immediately. We went home and I spent the rest of the weekend feeling these symptoms off and on. I wanted to be with David and was terrified to be alone, but I also couldn't tolerate having anyone near me. I sat in a fetal position in the basement of our townhouse with David sitting on the far side of the room. He tried to talk to me, but it only brought up more pain and panic. I rocked back and forth, which felt soothing. David had a hunch that the scene in the movie had brought this on, so he looked up the number of a rape crisis line. I called and they helped me calm down.

I started having panic attacks every day, several times a day—anytime I tried to leave the house. When my family called, I couldn't talk to them without panicking. I took that week off from work to try to get a handle on the panic.

I found a therapist and saw her for a few months, but I didn't feel safe with her. I felt as if she were reaching inside me, talking to parts of me that I didn't know yet and wasn't ready to acknowledge. It felt scary and hurried. However, she did help me devise a crisis management strategy. She taught me how to slow down my breathing when I felt panicky, and that simple suggestion made it possible for me to return to work. But each time she found a part and talked directly to it, I panicked and felt violated, and then our time was up.

My therapist and I decided that something traumatic must have happened to me when I was growing up. I told David this when I got home, and he was devastated. He cried. As I watched him cry, I felt scared and at the same time irritated. "Why are you crying?"

"Because this is the end of our relationship as we know it."

I was mad at him for crying. This new realization hadn't really sunk in yet, and I certainly didn't want to believe that it was going to change our relationship. I don't remember what I said to David that night; I just remember being irritated at his feelings and desperately trying not to feel similarly.

I wanted to go to a few therapy sessions and be back to normal. As I saw it, the panic attacks were the problem. What I really wanted was to stop having them. I genuinely thought I could do that. I didn't want to think about the past. But as the weeks went on and the panic attacks only increased, I asked my therapist to refer me to someone else. She was surprised. She had been thinking we were approaching the end of our work. I hadn't been telling her about the panic attacks I had after every session with her. At my insistence, she referred me to a psychiatrist.

It took me a little while to take the next step, but I eventually set up an appointment to see the psychiatrist. I was ashamed of needing to see a psychiatrist and didn't want anyone to know about it. I didn't want people to think there was something wrong with me.

Opening Doors

8

I sat nervously in the waiting area at the counseling center. Other people were coming and going, waiting for or leaving appointments, and I watched them all carefully. It took a lot for me to leave my house that morning for my appointment. I was terrified of having another panic attack, and I was scared of what was happening to me. I forced myself to go and felt mostly in a fog.

I wanted to disappear. Just being there in a waiting room was proof that something was wrong with me, that I was sick in some way. After a while, a man stepped out of one of the offices. He was of average height and had short brown hair with a touch of gray along the sides. His receding hairline left plenty of room for his gentle blue eyes. I looked into his eyes and got a good feeling about him.

I stood up as he approached me. He was dressed comfortably in brown slacks and a sweater vest over a casual shirt. I still felt a numbness inside but smiled to myself, thinking, *This is how psychiatrists are supposed to look.* He said, "I'm Doctor Mitchell Summer. Are you Ms. Trujillo?" He slowly and deliberately walked back to his office, and as I followed, I began to feel light-headed in that familiar way. Then the fuzziness took over and grew into a deeper numbness.

Each wall in his office was painted a different color. I felt joy deep inside and had to hold back from looking at the children's books stacked in the corner. A living room type of arrangement of furniture, with two chairs and a couch, took up most of his office, and farther back sat a desk covered with papers and a computer. "Sit wherever you want," he said. One of the chairs was black leather, large, and swiveling. A cup of hot tea sat next to it. *He doesn't mean that*, I thought instantly. *I can't sit in his chair.* I looked at the chair tucked behind the desk. *I can't sit at his desk, either. He doesn't mean what he says.* I silently considered my real options: the couch across from his black chair or the smaller leather chair, which would have put me sitting close to him. As I chose the couch, I wondered if I could trust Dr. Summer. *No*, came a small voice. I felt even more light-headed and disoriented.

He closed the door and moved to his seat, the big black leather chair that swiveled, and part of me said, *See?* He started talking, and even though I recognized the words, I couldn't connect them to each other. It was like being in a dream. Dr. Summer seemed very far away, at the end of a tunnel that was closing in on itself. I tried to make myself focus. He gave me a gentle, warm smile. I felt a little reassured and looked around his office.

There were books everywhere. I tried to read the titles but, as with his voice, I couldn't make sense of what they said. They were just words, as books often were to me, a bunch of words that didn't form into sentences, paragraphs, stories, cases, or articles. Eventually, I came to understand why I had such difficulty reading. Enduring the abuse of my childhood involved separating painful experiences up into little parts. Reading requires the opposite: taking separate pieces of information and putting them together to arrive at meaning. I was simply too practiced at not putting together pieces of a story.

Diplomas were displayed on one wall of Dr. Summer's office, too far away to see clearly, other than his name in big letters. *I have a lot of diplomas too, but not this many.* Suddenly I noticed that Dr. Summer wasn't talking. He was just sitting there, watching me study his office. My face started feeling hot, and I felt my nose and ears getting red. I realized that he was waiting for me to answer a question. My thoughts began to race, and then I became calm. "Why are all of your walls different colors?" I asked.

"What do you think about them?" he responded. They were pink, yellow, blue, and green. It felt jovial and light, a nice bright office. But I remained silent. "So, how can I help you?" he asked. That must have been his original question.

"I've been having some panic attacks," I heard myself say in a flat monotone I had used so many times before. I continued with no emotion, as though I was telling him what I'd had for breakfast. "I was seeing another therapist and she thinks I was abused when I was growing up, but I'm not sure. I can't see her anymore so she gave me your name. She said you supervised her work." I stopped talking and waited nervously. *I've told him too much,* came a young voice.

"What made her think you were abused when you were growing up?" he asked.

Don't tell him! He won't understand! "I've been having strange thoughts. I can see things in my head that don't make sense."

"I see," he said.

What do you see? It felt crowded in my head. There were too many voices.

After asking a few more questions about my previous therapist, he told me how he works with people. I don't remember any of what he said about his approach other than his rules. At first they seemed a bit heavy-handed, but I later came to understand that these rules created a structure in which I could safely do the work I needed to do: unravel my past.

"If you agree to work with me, you must come twice a week. If you miss a session, you will still have to pay for it. If you cannot make a session, you must let me know at least a day in advance, but you will still need to pay for it." This seemed harsh. I began to wonder if he was all about money, but I continued to listen. "You may be thinking about suicide, and I want you to know that this is normal." My mind raced again. My breath became hard to catch, and my head got even fuzzier. *How did he know?* He was right; I wished I could die. With every ounce of my being, I wanted to die. Sometimes it was a compulsion, and at other times it was just a sense of hopelessness. I didn't understand the difference between the two feelings; I just knew that I was miserable all the time.

Several times a day I was trapped in symptoms that I called a panic attack. All of a sudden I didn't feel safe. I would double over in severe abdominal pain, and a tightness in my chest would leave me gasping for air. I just wanted to lie in a corner in a fetal position, close my eyes, and wait out the pain and all the strange, horrific thoughts—thoughts that I was afraid to tell anyone about for fear that saying them would make them real. I later learned that this was physical and emotional pain from past traumas that was triggered and brought up again by experiences in the present that felt similar in some way, and that this is a common experience among those with a history of trauma.

I wanted it all to stop, and the only way I could think of to accomplish that was to die. I didn't want death to hurt; I just wanted to go to sleep and never wake up. I was planning it all the time. I thought about taking a bunch of pills and falling asleep forever. When driving alone, I considered driving my car into a tree along the highway. While running, I got urges to jump in front of a bus or truck. I thought I would probably die quickly that way. Although resisting these urges took an enormous amount of effort, I knew that if I killed myself I would hurt David beyond imagination, and I didn't want to hurt David. I just wanted the pain to stop.

The fact that Dr. Summer had brought up suicidal thoughts without me telling him about all of this gave me hope that he knew what he was doing. That hope was a huge relief. He went on with his rules: "While you're working with me, I need you to commit to not acting on any suicidal thoughts. We can set up a plan for when they come up and find people you can call to ask for help. You cannot break this commitment." *We'll see about that*, came a thought. I nodded in agreement. He continued, "I expect you to work hard at this. I commit to you that I will work hard with you. I will meet with you twice a week. I will help you as much as I can. You can call me when you're having a hard time, and whether it's the time of our appointment or not, I will call you back. I will commit to walking with you through this process if you commit to me that you will walk through this process with me." I was skeptical, and I wasn't convinced that all this talk of commitment was either believable or necessary. Nevertheless, I agreed. I felt I had no choice. I was panicking more and more, and even routine activities were hard to do.

I left Dr. Summer's office that day wondering whether he could help me. The longer I thought about it, the more hopeful I became. *He has all those diplomas, all those books, gentle eyes, a gentle smile, and a gentle manner despite his strict rules.* "Maybe this will help me," I said aloud as I drove back to my office. Although I hadn't—and couldn't have—said that deliberately to reassure and soothe the parts inside, it had that effect, slowing my racing thoughts so I could focus on work and what I had on my calendar for the day. I didn't know then that I had just switched from one part to another, or that I was beginning a process that would give me an understanding of how I was put together.

It was hard for me to go to my appointments because I didn't like leaving the relatively safe environment of my home or office. Everything outside of those safe places felt unpredictable and scary. I didn't tell Dr. Summer how terrifying the trip was; I just kept showing up and hoping that my work with him would help me. But for the first few months it didn't feel like we were getting anything done. My sessions with him felt superficial, our conversations inconsequential. We talked about problems at work or little issues at home.

I don't understand what I'm supposed to be doing, I often thought before a session. *I don't know how to do this.* Then more thoughts raced through. *I don't want to go. How is this helping? This costs so much. What is all of this for? How am I supposed to know what to do? He just sits there.* I felt helpless, panicky, and angry.

Later I learned that Dr. Summer was being very deliberate and thoughtful in his approach, and that we were getting quite a bit done without my knowing it. In those early sessions he was slowly and carefully getting me used to coming and going. He knew that panic can arise with transitions of any sort and was gradually exposing me to the notion that I could be safe in other places. Each time I successfully left one place and went to another, that feeling of safety grew in me and I became slightly more confident. I now know that many of my parts needed to learn this.

We never talked about agoraphobia; he just encouraged me to come to my sessions even when I didn't feel I could. He also encouraged me to go to work, to keep running, and to keep doing as many daily activities as possible. Just as important, he encouraged me to be gentle with myself even when I wasn't able to do these things.

Dr. Summer was also protective of me when things about my life worried him. My daily phone conversations with my mom and weekly calls with Mike had come to an abrupt halt when I started having panic attacks. I didn't know why, but I just didn't want to talk to them. Confused and hurt, they continued to call regularly, but David would simply say I wasn't available. I asked Dr. Summer about it, and even though he had otherwise encouraged me to keep up my daily habits, in this case he agreed that I should listen to my fears, however formless they might be.

During those early months, Dr. Summer was also building a relationship with me so that we could eventually do work that was more difficult. Through experiencing his consistency, I was learning that he was safe. I learned to trust his ideas—for example, that I was safe on the journey from his office to my home. He was caring and I could see it in his eyes. We were developing an environment in which I might come to trust him enough to talk about what I was remembering. *We'll see, we'll see...* kept running through my head. But with each session and every returned phone call, my trust grew.

One night, I had my worst panic attack yet. I had just gotten home from work. In the safety of our home, my thoughts raced uncontrollably and then the fuzziness came, as usual. But this time it didn't make me feel any calmer. I felt stabbing in my abdomen and doubled over in pain and terror. My chest became so tight I could barely breathe. It felt like I was going to die. Sobbing, I closed my eyes and worked very hard to get control of my head. I needed to think. I didn't want to slip into the black hole that loomed.

David was with me and asked, "What's happening? What can I do?" He wanted to hold me to help me feel safe and make the panic go away, but I couldn't tolerate having him near me.

I struggled to answer him and finally managed to say, "Call Dr. Summer." I lay in a fetal position, in pain and feeling fuzzy headed, with strange thoughts running through my mind: *Alex hurt me in the basement. Alex raped me.* I kept seeing scenes from this rape. Within the hour, Dr. Summer called back. I heard David telling him what was happening and then felt him hold the phone to my ear. Dr. Summer's voice was calm and reassuring, but my thoughts were hard to capture and the pain became more severe as I tried speak. "I feel pain. I can't stop the thoughts. I'm panicking." He calmly told me that I was safe. He reminded me that David was there, that David wouldn't hurt me, that David took good care of me. He asked me to take some slow, deep breaths. I inhaled and exhaled, inhaled and exhaled, and with each breath, the panic lessened.

"Clear your thoughts, Olga. Slow them down and clear them. Think about being in your home with David. You are safe now." As I listened, the pain lessened. The tension in my body loosened. My thoughts slowed and I felt numb. "How do you feel?" Dr. Summer asked.

"Better," I said softly, just above a whisper. In a small voice I had never heard before, I asked Dr. Summer, "Will David hurt me?" Dr. Summer reassured me that David loved me and wouldn't hurt me. He was right. David would never do anything but support and love me. I don't know how long I was on the phone with Dr. Summer that night, but when he hung up, my pain was gone, I was sitting up, and I had agreed to see him the next day. When I went in, rather than sit on the couch, I chose the smaller chair closer to him for the first time, thinking, *He called me back when I needed him.*

Several weeks later, our chatty conversations transformed into something deeper. When I arrived for my session, I plopped down in the smaller chair and admitted, "I don't know what I'm supposed to do here." He smiled. Looking back, I now think he had been waiting for me to trust him enough to admit that. He handed me a children's book, *There's a Nightmare in My Closet,* by Mercer Mayer. I looked at it and a younger voice asked, *What's this?* Then an older voice came up: *Is he kidding?* I sat there quietly with my thoughts, trying to figure out why he had given me a children's book to read.

Finally, Dr. Summer said, "Read it. I think it will help you understand our process." Feeling patronized, I opened the book. Surprisingly, my annoyance was instantly replaced by joy. I smiled a young smile and parts I didn't know existed looked excitedly at the book through my eyes. I could feel myself translating the English words into Spanish, which was odd because I hadn't spoken or thought in Spanish much at all since I was in college. But I didn't stay with that thought very long, and didn't mention it to Dr. Summer. The drawings were engaging and the story simple to follow.

A young boy is afraid of something in his closet. Every night he makes sure the closet door is closed tightly before going to bed, where he lies awake, gripping his popgun for protection. One night, his worst fears come true. He hears a nightmare creeping out of the closet toward him. He quickly turns on the light and shoots the nightmare with his popgun. The nightmare begins to cry. The boy, no longer afraid, comforts the nightmare by tucking him in bed and snuggling up next to him. They hear another noise and realize there must be another nightmare in the closet. But this time, the boy smiles. He's not worried. There isn't enough room in his bed for more nightmares.

In no time, I'd read the book all the way through. I put it down and changed the topic, telling Dr. Summer about something that happened that day. But something inside me insisted, *I need to tell him my nightmares. Not all my nightmares, but the thoughts I have.* I put down the book and a thought popped into my head: *Popi did something to me.* Then other thoughts followed: *Popi hurt me. Can we tell him? Popi hurt me. Can we tell him?* These thoughts bounced insistently through my mind. It felt like an internal conversation with a three-year-old. On the outside, I was still talking about work. But Dr. Summer seemed to notice that I was distracted and asked me if there was anything going on. I wanted to tell him, but I was terrified. Up to that time, I had only ever told him about present-day issues, never discussing my past. As I considered telling him, my head became fuzzy and unfocused and my chest felt tight as the parts I would come to know as Five, Seven, and Twelve came forward suddenly to protest. *We can't tell him. We can't tell anyone. It's our fault. He'll do it too.* I sat quietly, struggling to get out the words. I finally said softly, in a very young voice, "I think Popi did something to me. Something bad." Terror pulsed through my body. I braced myself for the barrage of questions and challenges that would surely come.

He considered me for a second. "Okay," he said.

"Does that make sense?" I asked, studying his expression carefully.

"Yes," he responded.

Relief washed over me in a way I'd never experienced before. I had told him, he listened, and I was okay. *Nothing bad happened. He believes me.* Even though the thought that Popi had hurt me didn't exactly feel connected to me, it had been terrorizing me, and I felt euphoric at releasing it. Maybe now it wouldn't haunt me anymore. Saying it was one of the most powerful things I ever experienced.

Furthermore, I had said it and hadn't been hurt in response. Dr. Summer didn't accuse me of lying. He had listened and believed me.

The relief didn't last long. A new thought came bouncing into my head to replace the one I had spoken. It was Twelve this time: *Alex hurt me. Alex did bad things to me. Alex hurt me.* My breathing became labored again. I saw short scenes of what happened in the basement on my birthday, but they were disjointed and didn't make sense to me. I felt frozen, too terrified to say aloud what I was thinking and seeing. The pain in my abdomen that always accompanied the panic came again, along with an urgency to tell—to have someone witness what had happened and believe me. After sitting silently for a while, tortured by thoughts, images, and pains, I said in a voice a little older than the one before, "Alex did bad things to me."

I searched Dr. Summer for a reaction, and he responded as before, with reassurance and kindness, saying, "Okay. What else are you thinking of?"

"Is this possible?" I asked him.

"Yes, sadly it is."

"I can see it in my head but it doesn't make sense."

"What do you see?" he wondered. I instantly felt fuzzy and stared off at the pictures in my mind: our apartment, the storage room, Alex, his friend Gary, them kicking me. I couldn't say it. Dr. Summer asked me again what I was seeing.

Finally, I said, "I feel pain." It was hard to catch my breath. I was back in the storage room.

"Olga," Dr. Summer said calmly but firmly. I came back part of the way, but was still half in the past. "Olga," he said more firmly. "Take a deep breath. You are safe here."

"I don't feel safe. It feels like it's happening now."

"I know," Dr. Summer responded, "but it's not. This is 1993. You are grown up, you live with David, and you are safe."

"I feel pain. The same pain that comes with panic attacks." I didn't understand why the pain was coming, why I was having these horrible thoughts. *Why?* kept running through my head. "Why is this happening? How can this be my life? How can this be true?"

Dr. Summer gently explained that when things happen that are too much for us to handle or understand, the mind instinctively protects us by storing the experience somewhere we cannot reach. He said that it sounded like that may have happened for me. The thoughts of Alex and the storage room came up again. I stared and flatly reported, as if talking about someone else, "Alex also did something bad to me. He and his friend Gary did it in the storage room at our apartment building." I felt no connection to the incident. Dr. Summer listened. He said that what I described was possible, and that he believed these things had happened to me.

Our session ended. Exhausted, I went to work. The last thing I wanted to do was leave the safety of Dr. Summer's office, get in my car, and drive downtown, but I focused on Dr. Summer's encouragement to keep my routine and reminded myself that it was safe. I couldn't focus, but I got through the day as best I could.

Later that week, on impulse, I called my mom. It had been months since we'd talked. Fresh from having said my scary thoughts aloud and having someone believe me, I was hopeful to have this same experience with her. I told her about my panic attacks and that I was seeing a therapist, then said, "I'm remembering things that Popi and Alex did to me." I gave her a sketchy outline of what I remembered, then held my breath and waited.

"I'm not surprised," she said casually, not missing a beat. "Popi was a hard man. And don't you remember that Alex was arrested when he was sixteen for raping that eight-year-old girl? He did that in the storage room too." There was no outrage, no worried questions—no emotion at all. It was surreal. But it was a huge relief to have her confirm what I was remembering. For that I was very grateful. We chatted a little while longer, talking about her workday.

I was still struggling with my emotions from that conversation when Mike called. I picked up. "Mom tells me you're remembering things that happened when we were little." He said that he also remembered my father beating my mother, and him and Alex. Even though he didn't remember Popi raping me, he wasn't surprised. I told him that I was also starting to remember what Alex did to me in the basement, but then Mike protested, saying, "You're killing me! I don't want to hear any more." His words were concerned, but his voice sounded angry. His words didn't match his tone. I didn't tell him anything else I remembered, but did let him know that I needed to focus on my therapy, my work, and my relationship with David, and that this was why I wasn't calling him as often. Mike said he understood.

In the next week or so, I pieced together the memory of being raped by Alex and Gary. Spitting mad, I was finally able to call Alex to confront him: "I remember you and Gary raping me in the storage room of our apartment building!"

"I never did that to you," he said, sounding genuinely surprised and a little scared.

"Yes, you did! Mom believes me. I also know you were arrested for raping an eight-year-old girl. I hate you and never want to talk to you again!" I heard more denials as I hung up the phone. That day, Alex called everyone in our extended family that he could reach—cousins, aunts, and uncles—to tell them that I was spreading lies about him.

•   •   •

The more Dr. Summer listened and reassured me, the more I trusted him. The more I trusted him, the more I told him about the thoughts, even though they were disjointed and seemed all over the place. I'd jump from thoughts about what my father did to me to thoughts of what Alex did. I would remember the experiences stored in a certain room inside me but not know why. I'd have pain but not know why. I had a hard time believing the thoughts were true and really didn't want the terrible stories I was piecing together to be my past. After months of this, I was flooded with thoughts, pain, and images that came up and poured out uncontrollably.

Although this information had reached my consciousness, I still couldn't feel connected to it. Dissociation kept the stories at a distance and helped me avoid being immobilized by panic attacks, but I didn't like being so numb all the time. I felt like I had been numb most of my life, and now I craved being able to have real feelings: the joy, the sadness, and everything in between. The problem was, the memories were simply too horrible and terrifying to feel all at once. I was stuck. In Dr. Summer's office, overwhelmed with all the thoughts, I often either stared blankly while telling him about a memory or fell silent, my eyes flickering back and forth so rapidly I couldn't keep them open.

One day Dr. Summer proposed that we try hypnosis as a way of allowing me to report what I was remembering while keeping a safe distance from the information so I wouldn't need to dissociate. I agreed. Under hypnosis, Dr. Summer helped me make a plan for handling the memories. To my relief, the thoughts slowed down. Hypnosis felt like a deeper sense of dissociation, but afterward I could always remember what happened.

Telling Dr. Summer what I was remembering without dissociating was a big accomplishment for me. But it didn't mean I was able to fully accept and connect to the experiences. I still felt distant from the information, as though the attacks hadn't really happened to me. Over the next several months, I simply reported thought after thought, mostly about things that Popi and Alex had done. I later learned that it was easier for me to remember what my father and Alex had done to me than what Mike had done because I had never felt close to them.

I came to understand intellectually that my mind used dissociation as a way to protect me from knowing things. Dr. Summer repeatedly explained, "If you had woken up every morning and knew that later that day or evening you would be abused, you would have killed yourself." I would always nod, as if in agreement. It all made sense in a theoretical way, but I could not and did not want to truly understand or accept what had happened to me. As more thoughts came up between sessions, I called Dr. Summer in the evenings more often. He always called back.

David continued to support me as best he could. He bought and read countless books on healing from childhood sexual abuse. He regularly attended a support group for partners of survivors of abuse. He helped me get to and from work. At the subway platform on our way to work together, if the train arrived full of people, I'd feel a catch in my chest and tell David that I couldn't get on. He would wait with me the ten minutes it took for another train to arrive, and if there was enough room, I'd get on, with him standing right behind me. It was comforting to have him there. I didn't know it then, but having someone safe there relieved my fear of being attacked from behind. As we got closer to work, inevitably the trains became even more crowded. I felt a pressure in my chest as if someone were sitting on me, my thoughts began to chase each other, the pain in my abdomen and back returned, and I felt as if I were going to jump out of my skin. David held on to me, almost in an attempt to keep me in the present. Knowing it was him helped me make it to our station, but I'd arrive at work exhausted from the journey.

As I became increasingly sensitive to crowds, David and I decided to start driving to work. It wasn't a hard decision, since my position at the Department of Justice afforded me a free parking spot. Sometimes David left work to drive me to and from my appointments with Dr. Summer. He chose to work the same hours I did so we could drive home together. He was devoted to my recovery and helped me in every way he could conceive of. I didn't tell Dr. Summer that I stopped taking the train. It was the kind of thing he would have been concerned about and challenged me on. He wanted me to feel safe, but he also thought that accommodating my fears was increasingly limiting my activities.

To keep up with the pace of my new memories, Dr. Summer added a session so I was seeing him three times a week. The more I told him, the more memories came up, and I was powerless to stop or slow down the thoughts. It felt as if parts of me were thinking, *We've waited long enough. Someone has to know this.* The flood of thoughts got worse, but I still felt disconnected from the memories. Even though they haunted me at work, at home, and in my sleep, I didn't want to own them and face the fact that this was my life. As much as I wanted to fully experience an authentic, full life, I was also desperate to hold on to the success I had created for myself—a life that was happy, orderly, safe, and secure.

I told Dr. Summer about my ongoing frustration: "I come in and tell you all these thoughts, but I don't know what to do with all of this information. I don't know what it all means or where I'm going with it."

Dr. Summer looked at me for a minute and asked me if I was annoyed or irritated. I said I was. I had been seeing him for many months, now three times a week, and I felt worse than when I began. "How is this helping me?"

Dr. Summer explained once again that he believed I was remembering real abuse that happened to me when I was growing up, that the thoughts were memories frozen in time by a dissociative process. We were piecing together a clear picture of what had happened to me so we could put my memories in their proper place: the past. He explained that the pain was my body remembering what had happened. He had explained the process many times before, just like this, but I still didn't understand. The words wouldn't connect. I asked, "How can I be a lawyer, be married? How can I be functioning if all this happened to me? I don't understand."

Before I started having panic attacks, I thought I'd had a happy childhood that I just didn't remember very well. I remembered doing things at the community center, at school, and with friends, but not much about our home life. I knew my father was strict and that he died when I was eleven. I didn't like Alex very much but thought it was because he always broke things and caused my mom stress. I had a better relationship with Mike but felt he was selfish and took advantage of me. Mike often asked for favors that seemed simple but would then grow. For example, he'd ask if I could take him to the airport, then say, "Oh, I forgot to tell you that the flight is at 6:00 a.m. and my friends Tim and Joe are coming too. You'll need to go get them at their houses." When I finally objected, he would call me a bitch—his usual term for me when I wasn't doing what he wanted—and hang up on me in disgust.

I thought I'd had a close, even loving relationship with my mom. After all, for years we'd talked every day, but recently I'd begun to feel uneasy about some things in our relationship, particularly that I did a lot for her and bought her lots of things she wanted, but she rarely did anything for me.

All of my family issues aside, I knew that I was happy, successful, and married to a great guy and had a promising career. All of this was true, but it wasn't the whole truth. Yet I desperately held on to the fantasy.

"You need to connect the thoughts to you," Dr. Summer finally recommended. He gave me another book, *A Wizard of Earthsea*, by Ursula K. Le Guin, and said, "I think this may help you understand what I mean."

9

I drove myself home after the therapy session and put the book down on the foyer table, along with my briefcase. I was always bringing work home. Because my ability to concentrate and read wasn't very good, my work inevitably spilled over into my evenings and weekends. As I went upstairs to hang up my work clothes and put on sweats, I kept thinking about my session with Dr. Summer. *He knows I have trouble reading. Why did he give me a book to read? Why this fantasy book? I don't like fantasy stories.* I was annoyed but at the same time a bit curious. I had been feeling so lost in my sessions lately. Although I was normally good at everything I tried, my work with Dr. Summer made me feel like I was spinning my wheels and sinking deeper. It was hard not knowing what I needed to do. It left me feeling vulnerable. I was afraid Dr. Summer would figure out I wasn't as smart as people thought I was.

David wasn't going to get home for another few hours. I thought about making dinner or getting some work done, but my curiosity about the book got the better of me. I was intrigued about why Dr. Summer thought it was perfect for me now and what it would show me about my path, so I sat down on the couch to read. The first surprise was that I could concentrate on the book very well. I was able to focus. Then I was startled to find myself internally interpreting the story into Spanish, even though I never had reason to speak it anymore. I later realized that the story was captivating for all the ages inside me, and all of us were reading it together.

In short, the story is about Ged, a boy with the potential for being a great magician. The youngest of eight boys in his family, he was born on the island of Gont, known for its goat thieves and wizards. His mother died shortly after his birth, so he was raised by his father, a bronzesmith, who neglected him. His mother's sister, a witch, took care of Ged as an infant, but as soon as he could modestly fend for himself she too neglected him. So Ged spent his youngest years alone, while his older brothers farmed the land and worked in trades. When at home, he was repeatedly told how useless he was.

The story felt familiar to me in ways I couldn't explain. I instantly felt a connection with Ged. I could feel his story inside me. *Useless, useless, useless* ran through my head. I read on with a hunger for the message Dr. Summer thought was buried, waiting for me in the story. I lost track of time and was still reading when David got home from work.

I didn't want to stop reading, but I put the book down, went to the foyer, and hugged David. I asked him about his day. As he responded, I noticed how tired he looked and worried about it: *I'm making him tired. He worries so much about me. Is this too much for him? Is he going to leave me?* Lost in my thoughts and worries, I didn't listen to what David was saying about his day. I realize now that I often didn't listen to David. Our lives had become about my healing. And I was so distracted most of the time that David as a person with separate thoughts and feelings had become invisible to me. He was my husband, but mostly he was helping me get through a crisis. There was no room in my world for David's fears, feelings, thoughts, and worries. I tolerated them, but I didn't embrace them or him beyond what I needed. Despite all that, David never complained about how drastically our lives had changed and how much I had changed since we got married.

I showed David the book, and while we made dinner together, I told him about my session. "Dr. Summer thinks this book will help me understand what I'm supposed to be doing."

David looked at the book and asked, "Are you able to read it?"

"Yes. Isn't that weird?"

"It is, but it's great. Maybe it means you're getting better." I noticed a hopeful tone. After dinner, instead of watching TV as we usually did, I picked up the book again and David read as well. He always had a stack of books waiting for him.

Ged, at age thirteen, saved the island of Gont from an attack by a neighboring island that was part of the Kargad Empire. The villagers had heard about the destruction the Kargs were wreaking on other island towns and prepared themselves for a futile battle: a few goat herders against many warriors. As the Kargs approached Ged's village, in desperation he created a spell to surround the attackers with a great fog to disorient them. When Ged spoke the spell, the fog formed and the attackers were unable to see anything around them. The villagers, who knew the land well, weren't disoriented by the fog and were able to defeat the Kargs.

After saving the island, Ged caught the attention of a wise old wizard, Ogion the Silent, who told Ged's father that Ged had the power of a wizard but desperately needed knowledge, as those who have great power but limited knowledge are vulnerable to the darkness. He offered to take Ged with him to teach him. His father reluctantly agreed and Ged went with Ogion.

As I read, *darkness* bounced around in my head ominously.

Ogion was a patient man. Ged revered him for all he'd heard about Ogion's abilities to speak to mountains and quiet earthquakes. He thought Ogion would teach him spells and incantations and ways of having power over others. Ogion, however, had a different style of teaching. He took many walks with Ged and didn't talk much except to comment on flowers and scenery. Ogion was so unassuming, so down-to-earth, that Ged started to challenge him impatiently.

I thought of Dr. Summer: *I have to learn his way of teaching me. Is this what I'm supposed to learn? Am I like Ged, vulnerable to the darkness because I lack knowledge?* I didn't know what the darkness was, but I knew something scary and dark was inside of me.

I read on that night and lost track of time. I was startled when David said he was going to bed soon and asked if I would be up much longer. *I don't want to stop,* came a voice from inside. It was 11:00 p.m. I said I would read for a little longer and then come to bed.

I continued to read more about Ged's life with Ogion. Ged kept asking Ogion when he was going to teach him wizardry. Ogion said his lessons had already begun. Frustrated, Ged couldn't see what he was supposed to be learning by walking around in the woods and being silent.

My thoughts went to my relationship with Dr. Summer: *I have lost patience. Dr. Summer wants us to go slow, and I want to hurry. Is this part of what he wants me to understand?* I realized that it was 12:30 in the morning and David had gone to sleep. I had been so engrossed in the book that I didn't hear him wish me goodnight. I wondered if he was mad at me and woke him up just to ask if he was. He said he wasn't, and that he just hadn't wanted to interrupt me. I changed and went to bed but woke up early to go downstairs and read more.

Ogion knew that Ged was impatient. He wanted to teach him that wizardry is best used only at times of great need. But Ged was restless and very eager to learn. Although Ged loved Ogion, when given the choice to stay with Ogion and learn his way or go to a school for wizards, Ged chose to leave.

I kept thinking about my own impatience with Dr. Summer. I believed he could help me. I just didn't know how.

At school, Ged developed a reputation for learning quickly and soon reached the top of his class, second only to an older student named Jasper. One day Ged, anxious to prove his power in front of the other students and Jasper, spoke aloud the incantation to summon the dead. In doing so, he inadvertently raised a faceless, shadowy figure. This shadow of great evil attacked Ged and almost killed him.

My thoughts wandered. *Does Dr. Summer want me to take the memories more seriously? Is this what he wants me to learn?*

I heard David upstairs getting dressed to go running with me. At this point, I was halfway through the book and reluctantly put it down and changed into my running clothes. We ran our usual route and got ready for work, but throughout I was distracted by the story and what it meant for me. *What does Dr. Summer want me to learn? That I need to go slowly? That he is wise like Ogion?* I was so desperate to find the answers to these questions. It didn't occur to me that my quest for the meaning of the book was hurried and distant, just like my approach to therapy: hurry and remember, report the memories to Dr. Summer, and distance myself from them. I had only superficially accepted what I was remembering and how I survived.

After work, David and I drove home together. As he talked about his day, I only half listened, thoughts of the book and what I was supposed to learn from it swimming in my head. I waited until he was done before I started talking about the book again. I gave him a summary of the story and my ideas about what I was supposed to learn. He thought my ideas were plausible.

"Do you want to read again tonight?" I asked him excitedly. "I was hoping to finish the book tonight. I have a session with Dr. Summer tomorrow, and I want to discuss it with him." David agreed. At home, I went right up to change into my sweats and David fixed dinner. I settled into the couch and began reading again.

The wizard headmaster of the school intervened to save Ged from the shadow of evil, who fled the island, but the great wizard gave his life, for the shadow was too powerful. The experience was humbling for Ged, who lost a year of schooling while recuperating in the hospital. Once he was healthy enough to reenter school, he studied earnestly but with a solemn approach. He had lost most of his confidence but stayed at school for several more years, studying to eventually receive his wizard's staff. He worked hard not to think of the shadow, although it often came up in his mind.

I saw myself in Ged before he had raised the shadow. I realized that I thought I was something special too. I went to law school, passed the bar, and worked at a big law firm and then at the Department of Justice. I was young to be in such an important position. I was at times cavalier, condescending, and arrogant. I wondered whether Dr. Summer wanted me to be more humble, or whether I wasn't respecting the process. I wondered if it could be that the memories were within reach for years and I just hadn't wanted to face them, like Ged didn't want to think of the shadowy darkness.

I read on. Upon graduating from school, Ged was assigned a wizard position on the island of Pendor. There his task was to help the residents solve their problem with six dragons that constantly threatened them. He sailed to the island home of the dragons, where he easily defeated the five youngest dragons before confronting the oldest, most dangerous one. After a lengthy battle, he gained power over the dragon and ordered him to stay on his home island and never again go to the island of Pendor. From that day forward, the dragon left the islanders in peace.

Never free from the threat of the shadow that still pursued him, Ged began a nomadic journey, sailing from island to island and never resting anywhere for long. At times the shadow almost caught him outright or tricked him into a trap. He was seduced by the shadow to get involved with evil sorcerers who promised him great power and riches. Each time, he barely escaped.

Finally, in desperation and exhaustion, he sailed home to Ogion to seek his advice. Ged confessed his foolish mistake in raising the powerful shadow and asked for Ogion's advice in defeating it. As they sat and puzzled through it together, Ogion suggested that Ged turn and face the shadow rather than run from it.

This hit me hard. My thoughts raced. It was hard to focus on any one thought. I had trouble catching my breath. I closed the book for a moment and closed my eyes. I tried very hard to focus. *Face the shadow rather than run from it—is this what Dr. Summer wants me to do? But I am facing the darkness in my life. I'm remembering all sorts of awful things.* I asked David what he thought. "That could be what Dr. Summer wants you to learn, but aren't you doing that already?" he asked.

"I thought so," I answered.

"Did you finish the book?"

"No, not yet."

"Well, why don't you keep reading and see if that's it?"

I sat there silently. I felt scared. Finally I said, "I don't want to face it anymore."

David gave me a reassuring smile. "I know, honey. But you can do it." I didn't feel very capable—just scared. I sat there for a few more minutes before opening the book again.

Ged did just what Ogion suggested. He turned around and started chasing the shadow. At one point he got close enough to grab it, but opened his hands to find nothing there. He couldn't understand the nature of the shadow, what it was made of, and why it wanted him. But he continued, traveling vast distances, past many islands, in pursuit of the shadow. Finally, at the edge of the sea, where water turns to sand, Ged caught up with the shadow and it turned to face him.

The shadow first took the form of his father, then an enemy, then finally Ged himself. Ged realized that the shadow was his own dark side, not something separate from him. He knew what to do. He embraced it and it entered him, and in that moment he became whole.

"Light and darkness met, and joined, and were one."

My thoughts settled and the image of Ged embracing the shadow struck me. Over and over again, I thought, *He embraced it.* I closed the book and began to cry. David held me.

● ● ●

I saw Dr. Summer the next day. "I read the book," I said almost immediately after sitting down in the smaller chair.

"Oh," Dr. Summer said. "What do you think?"

"It's a good story. I can see the parallels to my life."

"How so?" he asked.

"Well, I can see how I have a shadow in the form of the night-mares and thoughts. I can see how I've been running away from them all my life—how all the activities, all the jobs and schooling have helped me avoid the nightmares and thoughts that I've been having for years."

Dr. Summer listened quietly, then finally said, "Is there anything else you see from this story?"

"I can see how I'm like Ged. How I've spent so much of my life trying to get respect and power. I think that's why I went to law school. I think that's why I like the position I'm in now. It proves that I'm good, that I'm smart and deserve respect. I can also see how I haven't treated people well because of my sense of pride or power."

I gave him a couple more examples, but I felt a pressure inside to talk about the bigger issue the book had raised. I could tell he was waiting for me to raise it as well. I sat silently for a while, my thoughts racing.

"I get it, you know."

"You get what?" Dr. Summer asked with a bit of a smile.

"I get what I have to do in here. I have to do what Ged did. I have to accept the dark side of my life."

Dr. Summer considered me for a minute and smiled again. "Yes," he said softly.

I started crying gently, and then harder. I'm sure Dr. Summer could barely understand what I was saying through the tears: "I don't want to, Dr. Summer. I don't know how. I'm afraid it will kill me."

"Ged thought that, too," Dr. Summer reminded me.

"What if I'm not strong enough?"

Dr. Summer sat silently, a witness to my fear and grief. Suddenly, my thoughts were clear and certain: *This is my life. The thoughts I've been telling him happened to me. The memories are all a part of me.* I continued to cry.

Dr. Summer said, "If you weren't strong enough, you wouldn't be here. You wouldn't have understood what you had to do. You'd still be running from the shadow, from the darkness."

I drove home afterward with a deep sense of foreboding. I finally understood what I needed to be doing in therapy and was terrified. Overwhelmed by the fear of what was inside of me, the familiar fuzziness filled my head. I felt calm, then numb again.

10

At my next session, I fell into the chair in resignation and again confessed, "I don't want to do this." *A Wizard of Earthsea* had helped me understand what I was supposed to be working on, but I still didn't want to own the memories. "How could I even function today if all of this happened to me?" I pleaded, wishing Dr. Summer would tell me that he'd been wrong, that all of those thoughts didn't belong to me.

Dr. Summer reminded me gently, "When you were attacked, your mind went far away so you could survive. Some people describe this as an out-of-body experience. Your mind creatively and instinctively protected you by dissociating from the violence and terror. When you talk about the thoughts in your head, you have a flat demeanor like you're talking about someone else. Doesn't it feel that way to you?"

"Yes. It doesn't ever feel like I'm talking about me. It doesn't feel like it happened to me."

I was on the edge of the cliff and didn't trust that I would survive a fall into the darkness of my past. But the image of Ged embracing his shadow was powerful, and it stayed with me. I thought about what I was remembering for a brief minute. I tried not to dissociate. I said in resignation, "It's me. I was three years old," and started to cry softly. For the first time, I connected myself to the thoughts about the three-year-old being raped. I could feel that it was me.

Dr. Summer had explained repeatedly how, as a child, I had separated into parts to survive the abuse that I was remembering in segmented pictures and thoughts. I struggled to grasp what this meant. Over and over, I thought, *I needed to separate into parts in my head. I needed to separate into parts in my head*, but I couldn't make sense of this. They were just words that didn't come together into something meaningful. A thought came up. I chased it and was able to hold on to it long enough to ponder it: *I could not know this or something bad would have happened.*

As I continued to focus silently on the thoughts of being hurt when I was three, I started to feel light-headed and dizzy. I was scared but kept listening to the thoughts. My thoughts were now in Spanish. *I'm Three*, came a thought. *I lived in the house on 12th Street with Mame and Popi. My name is Olguita. I was hurt by Popi.* The scene of the first rape I remember suddenly came up to the surface, followed closely by terror and pain. Dr. Summer watched me closely from his chair. "What's happening?"

"It's Popi I see hurting me." My breath grew shallower and harder to catch. The pain in my lower abdomen and back suddenly got stronger. "Dr. Summer, the panic is coming! Help me!"

Calm and commanding, Dr. Summer said, "Slow your breathing, Olga." I stared off, listening to his voice. Three, who had been trained to do as she was told, followed his instructions. "Slow, deep breaths. Now again, another deep breath. You're safe. It's 1994 and no one is going to hurt you. You live with David, who loves you very much. You work at the Department of Justice and they value your work. You are big now and you are safe."

I clung to his words as if they were a lifeline and I was drowning. Slowly, I took one deep breath after another. The pain in my abdomen eased. The more Dr. Summer talked, the calmer I got. After about twenty minutes of this kind of guidance, I was able to bring myself back to the present moment, in his office.

Dr. Summer gently told me that our session had gone over by about fifteen minutes and reminded me that someone else was waiting to meet with him. I was still in pain, exhausted, and shaking, and very vulnerable. I felt disoriented by the three-year-old part that had just surfaced and was struggling to regain control over my mind and body. Dr. Summer explained that when the pain and panic came up, we had to stay with that and help me find some relief, but in the process we had run past our usual time. Perhaps sensing that I didn't understand him and wasn't yet ready to go back to work, he proposed a solution: "I'm going to walk you over to a part of the office where there won't be many people. I want you to wait there, and I'll check in with you between patients. I have an opening in a few hours. We can finish our work then. Does that sound okay to you?"

Silently, I hung on every word. I focused on Dr. Summer and worked hard to make sense of it all. I felt like I had after that first rape I remember, like I was hiding under the bed praying, my head full of cotton. The Hail Mary ran through my thoughts over and over in Spanish, and I wondered why I was thinking in Spanish. I felt beat up and was still having pain that reminded me of the rape. I was exhausted by everything that was going on and just wanted to lie down and close my eyes. Dr. Summer gave me a reassuring look that made me think he could understand my struggle. As he escorted me to the secluded waiting area, I told him, "I feel pain."

"That's the part of you that Popi hurt. She wants you to know how he hurt you," he said very softly. He reminded me that he would be back to check in with me between sessions and that we could meet again later in the day. He walked me to a chair in the corner of the room, an alcove where I'd have one wall behind me and another to my side. I tearfully thanked him and thought, *He knows so much about me. He cares. He's going to help us.*

After a little while I was able to compose myself enough to find a restroom down the hall. In the mirror, my eyes looked red and puffy from crying. That was as expected. But I was surprised to notice that I looked older than I should be. I didn't expect to be dressed up for work. I looked down at my shoes and feet, and they didn't look like mine. Alarmed, I splashed my face with cold water and looked again. The reflection didn't show who I thought I was.

As I washed my hands, they didn't look like mine either. They looked too big. I was wearing rings. It was all very startling and confusing. I felt a little panicky and didn't want to think about it too hard. Disoriented, I banged into the doorway on my way out of the restroom and thought, *Why is this door so small? Why am I taking up so much space in this hall? Whose hands are those? Whose eyes and face was I seeing?* My thoughts began to race and I started having trouble catching my breath. Then I felt the fuzziness in my head, followed by calmness, and finally numbness.

I asked the receptionist if I could use a phone in privacy and called my office. I was still feeling unable to think clearly, and I'm sure I sounded flat. I let them know I wouldn't be in that day. The people I worked with already knew some of what was going on with me because I had asked for an accommodation under the Americans with Disabilities Act to be able to leave during the day for therapy. Even though my boss and coworkers knew I struggled with panic attacks that stemmed from abuse I had suffered as a child and that I was seeing a psychiatrist for help, I was always so composed around them that it must have been hard to understand what I was going through.

I called David and let him know that I was still at Dr. Summer's office. I explained what I could remember and how I was starting to connect the memories to me and he asked me how I was doing. I could feel the emotion in my throat, and tears started to fill my eyes again. Even though it made me feel too vulnerable, I needed to tell David what was happening. I needed to not feel alone. I finally answered quietly, "I've had a really hard session. I panicked and it feels like memories are very close to the surface. I don't feel like myself and I'm scared." I hid my face as tears streamed down. David asked if I wanted him to come get me. "No, thanks. I'm waiting for another session with Dr. Summer. I'll probably be okay to drive home later."

"Are you okay otherwise?" This was David's way of asking if I was feeling suicidal. He worried about my suicidal thoughts and planning and wanted to be able to ask me about it, but he couldn't use the word "suicidal" without getting scared and crying. We had agreed that he would use the word "otherwise" as a kind of code.

"I'm okay. No thoughts or anything. I'm so consumed with this memory it feels like there's no space for that in my head right now."

He sighed in relief. I felt sad for burdening him with so much worry. As we said good-bye, he told me, "Call me if you need me to pick you up."

"I will. I promise not to get into the car if I feel that way. I'll stay here and call you if those feelings come up." David and I had talked a lot about what I would do if I felt suicidal. I promised not to act on the feelings and instead call him or Dr. Summer. If neither of them were available, I would move on to a list of friends that I carried with me. David and I had talked to these friends and asked for their support, explaining that if I called I would tell them where I was and what I was feeling or planning. We told them that they only needed to tell me that they cared about me. They could remind me what year it was and remind me of my promise to David and Dr. Summer that I wouldn't act on any plans to kill myself. With all of that clearly spelled out, several friends agreed to be on my list, and I did end up calling some of them. Each time, they helped me ride out the compelling feelings.

I went back to the alcove to wait. Dr. Summer did exactly as he said he would. He showed up to check on me between his sessions, and each time I saw him, I was more in control inside. Three was still there but was fading back. Meanwhile, I held on to Dr. Summer's words: *This is 1994. I am safe. Dr. Summer will check in with me between sessions, and we'll meet again after a few hours.* I felt myself trusting him more and more.

Around 3:00, Dr. Summer came to get me. I was still feeling numb and fuzzy, but much improved from earlier in the day. I felt calmer and safer still as I entered his office. Slumped in the chair, I felt small, as if its adult size didn't fit me. I didn't seem to take up as much space as I had before.

"You did very good, hard work today. How are you feeling?" he asked.

"I'm exhausted," I said very softly. "I feel like I've been run over by a truck. Everything hurts."

"That's because of the adrenaline that was pumping through you when you panicked. It must be leaving your body now." We were silent together for a minute before he asked, "Do you know what happened before the panic and the pain?" I thought for a little while and felt my head filling with cotton. I couldn't focus my eyes. Dr. Summer stopped me right away. "How are you feeling right now? What are your thoughts?"

It took me a few minutes to answer. "My thoughts are in Spanish. It takes me a little while to translate them back into English."

Dr. Summer nodded. "That makes sense." Then there was silence. I didn't want to know why it made sense to him. "What else are you feeling?"

"I feel distant. I don't feel much of anything, really."

"I want you to pay attention to this feeling. You are dissociating."

"Okay. I can pay attention to it, but I feel this way a lot."

"I understand, but remember that you want to try to stop using dissociation as a way to avoid your feelings. You've told me that you want to feel, as painful as it sometimes is. With bad feelings also come good feelings. That is where we want to go: where you can feel pure joy and profound happiness."

"Okay."

"So for now, I want you to notice when you feel this way. Then we'll try to figure out what happened just prior that led you to dissociate. Then we'll discuss strategies to change those things so that you won't need to dissociate."

"Okay," I said, but it was too much for me to hold on to, and I didn't even remember that we had already discussed this plan. I was exhausted, but there was one more thing I needed to say: "I had this weird experience in the bathroom today. I didn't look like me in the mirror. I felt taller than I should be, and my hands didn't look like they belonged to me." Fear started rising up.

Dr. Summer leaned forward in his chair and firmly said, "That makes sense to me. It's nothing to be afraid of."

"It makes sense to you?" I asked. It comforted me to know he understood. If it made sense to him, I wasn't alone.

"Yes."

We were both silent for a moment. "It's nothing to be afraid of?" I asked, wanting reassurance.

"Right." Silence hung over us again, then Dr. Summer said, "So let's talk about this morning. How were you feeling before you panicked?"

"It started when I could see it was me who was being raped by Popi. Then I felt terror." As I was telling him, I could feel myself becoming increasingly calm and distant.

"Can you tell that you're dissociating now?"

"Yes. But it's too hard to go there, Dr. Summer. It hurts and it's very scary."

"Let's just try to contain this memory until our next session. I'll ask you to take a deep breath and close your eyes if you feel safe enough. Then I'll use hypnosis to create a container in your mind where this memory and any related feelings, emotions, and thoughts can reside until our next session. How does that sound?"

Without fully grasping the full meaning of what he was saying, I agreed because I trusted him. I wanted the pain to go away. And more than anything, I wanted to be happy.

I took a deep breath, then followed Dr. Summer's instructions as he said, "Close your eyes. Go deeper and deeper. The feelings, emotions, and thoughts from this incident shall gather. Say yes when all has gathered."

I could feel and see in my head short scenes of the rape and the related thoughts and emotions as if in color. Once I could feel them all in the center of my mind, I softly said, "Yes."

"That's good. Now let's picture a container: a large, round container. Let's make it big enough to fit all the memories, pictures, feelings, and emotions. Can you see it?"

"Yes." I pictured a huge yellow industrial trash can in my head. It had a hazard symbol on the side. There were chains around it, with padlocks to seal it tight.

"Let's open it up, then, and put the memories, pictures, feelings, and emotions inside. Let me know when you are done by saying yes."

In my head I pictured a three-year-old Olguita stuffing black plastic trash bags into the container. Once they were all in, I softly said, "Yes."

"Okay, now that all the memories, pictures, feelings, and emotions are inside, close the lid and lock the container. When you are done, say yes."

I saw Olguita closing the lid, jumping on top of it to make sure it was closed, and then locking the chains. "Yes."

"That's very good. These memories, pictures, feelings, and emotions shall stay inside this container until five minutes after the beginning of our next face-to-face session. When I count from three to one and say that word to bring you back, that word being 'open,' you will awake and be in your normal waking state. Three, two, one, open."

I opened my eyes and felt better, exhausted but relieved of a burden. The pressure to tell and the weight of the emotions had been with me for weeks. Now that I'd told what had happened, the burden lifted a bit. After a few minutes I had my bearings and told Dr. Summer I was ready to go. He looked at me very closely and agreed.

I thanked him and we shook hands. I remember his warm grip. With an understanding smile, he said, "Take good care of yourself today."

At home, I changed into my sweats and lay on the couch to watch TV. As long as it wasn't edgy or violent, TV helped me shut my mind down, avoid the worries I had about work and David, and, in this case, stop thinking about my sessions that day. Later, when David got home, he made us dinner and sat with me as I told him what I remembered from the sessions. He listened intently and asked questions. I explained what I could.

David and I ate dinner on the couch. Afterward he washed dishes and I settled into the couch for the night. It had been months since I had slept in our bedroom on a regular basis. It had nothing to do with our room or David. Since I had begun therapy, when in any proper bed I would see images of all the different ways I was hurt in my bedrooms growing up. The images would rush into my mind and overwhelm me, and I'd wake in a panic. So I slept on the couch instead, and David, not wanting to leave me alone, slept on the floor of the living room. If I woke up in a memory, he was always right there to soothe my pain and panic and remind me that it was 1994. I can't remember how long we slept in the living room like this, but it must have been for at least six months.

●　○　●

As the weeks passed, I learned to identify when I dissociated. I knew that the thoughts I'd been having were about me, but panic still came up each time I allowed my mind to truly feel that it was me who was being attacked. And I still didn't know very much about the complex coping mechanism that had helped me survive my child-hood. It was as if my conscious mind wasn't strong enough yet to fully grasp that I had parts. I knew it superficially, but I didn't feel it all the way through. I just understood very clearly that we had to go slowly. Dr. Summer and I came up with a motto as a reminder: "Slow is good."

Some of the parts inside me were ready to come up and tell what had happened, but others didn't want me to know they even existed. I learned that when parts were in conflict with each other or didn't like what I was doing, I felt pain and panic. Dr. Summer encouraged me to pay attention to the parts and address the issues they raised, but to also challenge them and keep doing as many of my normal activities as I could.

I understood these things intellectually, the way I understand that the world is round or that gravity is a universal force. But it took me a long time to truly grasp what Dr. Summer had told me many times before: "To survive a violent childhood, you created aspects of your consciousness that held information about the violence away from you. That's why you remember it as if it happened to someone else. You have many ways of being you."

I often responded by asking how I could have done all that and not known it, to which he'd respond, "Your mind protected you. To do this, you had to be creative and intelligent. You are amazingly resilient." Dr. Summer was wonderful at reframing things. He explained my mind to me for a long time without using any diagnostic terminology at all. So instead of seeing myself as crazy or flawed, I could think of myself as strong and intelligent. My extraordinary system of parts had helped me develop as a person, make friends, and excel in school and sports.

During this time, I finally learned my diagnosis. Dr. Summer told me, "Because of the violence you endured and the trauma you suffered, you developed what is known as dissociative identity disorder, or DID, formerly known as multiple personality disorder. DID is a range of disorders involving dissociation and the creation of parts to protect you from severe trauma. In your situation, you were able to keep a central 'you' that's always present on some level. This central you is able to be aware of your other parts. Your parts are also able to know and interact with each other. This is called co-consciousness." He showed me the diagnostic definition from the fourth edition of the *Diagnostic and Statistical Manual of Mental Health Disorders* (known as the *DSM-IV*), published by the American Psychiatric Association.

The diagnosis shouldn't have surprised me, as we had been talking about my symptoms for so long. But it's easier to think you just have a bunch of parts inside. Everyone says things like "A part of me wants to go to the movies, but another part of me wants to just stay home." Using the term "part" made me feel normal. I knew I was a little different in that my parts were quite separate aspects of me. I knew my consciousness wasn't whole and knew that it was unusual to have some thoughts come to me in Spanish. I knew most people didn't experience terror and struggle to catch their breath when they were in benign situations. But we hadn't been calling this DID, so I'd been able to avoid fully accepting the implications of having these special parts.

I was shocked and terrified to hear Dr. Summer say I had what was formerly known as multiple personality disorder. *Is that like Sybil? Am I like the woman in* The Three Faces of Eve? My head began to spin. *What do I have inside of me? Is there a crazy person in there? What am I?* I felt like a freak. I was afraid to have anyone know. *I have a mental illness. People make fun of people like me.* Upon hearing my diagnosis, I stopped thinking of myself as smart, creative, or clever. Even though Dr. Summer had worked hard to help me understand that I had developed an amazingly adaptive survival technique, I no longer thought of it that way at all.

I was overwhelmed by fear and shame. The words *multiple personality disorder* echoed in my mind. I thought of all the ways people with multiple personalities were ridiculed and marginalized: *They're locked away in mental institutions. They are really sick. I'm not going to be the subject of people's jokes. I am a lawyer. I work at the U.S. Department of Justice.* The more I thought about it, the deeper my despair grew. *What would my boss do if she knew? They could take my security clearance away. I could lose everything.* My bosses could get access to my medical insurance records. I'd have to update them at some point to keep my ADA accommodation. They were going to find out eventually, one way or another. *What will they do? People at work like and respect me. I'm so young to hold my position. I'm a success. How will they treat me now?*

I wondered if my friends would stop talking to me now that I was officially "crazy." *What if they think I'll hurt their kids?* That was a devastating thought. Then I was struck by an even bigger fear, and it's strange how long it took to surface: *What will David do? Will he be afraid of me? Will he leave me? I can't make it without David.* I was terrified, afraid of losing everything that I had worked so hard to build for myself, everything that kept me safe and secure. *This can't be my life. It just can't be my life* ran through my head over and over again.

11

Although Dr. Summer told me that I was making significant progress, it seemed like everything was getting harder. At the office, I tried to avoid the strange thoughts and pictures in my head by focusing on work. But at home things were different. One day, within a half hour of getting home, three-year-old Olguita came close to the surface and showed me in graphic detail how Popi raped my mom and then me. I was in the kitchen cooking dinner with David—one of the rare days I had energy enough to cook.

David asked me if something was wrong, but saying it aloud would have made it real, so I stopped cooking and just stared off into space. I felt stuck in the memory of Popi's rapes. David tried to help by reminding me what year it was and letting me know that I was safe now. I could barely hear him. Three didn't want to listen to David and said, *I'm not sure I trust him. He could hurt me if he wanted to.* Not wanting to upset David any more than I had to, I didn't share those thoughts. Three showed me that Popi also raped me in my bedroom. I ignored the fact that I was remembering this in Spanish and tried to push the thoughts away because I just wanted to make dinner with David for once. But as I was learning, ignoring a part is never a good strategy.

Looking concerned, David asked, "What's going on inside?"

I looked at him and started crying. "I think I'm having flash-backs." By this time, I had found the courage to tell him about the diagnosis of DID and show him what it said in the *DSM-IV.* David wasn't surprised. I was so relieved and thought, *He knows, and he isn't afraid of me.*

In the kitchen that evening, he asked, "Can I help?"

I said, "No, I don't think so. I'm going to try to contain the flashbacks until I see Dr. Summer." I sat on the bottom step of the staircase just across from the kitchen. I closed my eyes, pictured the containers, and tried to have Three go into the container. It didn't work. Under hypnosis we had agreed that only one memory would be allowed to come out at a time, and not before the start of our next session. But my unruly thoughts had been breaking out lately. There was simply too much information and not enough time with Dr. Summer to get it all out. Eventually, we had to make the first container sit in another larger container, then another and another, like Russian nesting dolls.

The harder I tried, the angrier Three got, protesting, *Don't ignore me! You have to know this!* In my mind I saw my father kicking me in my stomach when I hid from him under my bed, and I felt the pain of his blows. Crying, I silently asked Three to stop showing me this. *I don't want to know this now! We agreed this won't happen outside Dr. Summer's office. Olguita, please wait until we see him again.* She responded, *No! We need to know this now,* and I felt a sharp, constant pain and pressure in my chest. I had to breathe harder and harder to get some air.

I was trying not to use dissociation to escape reality and worked especially hard not to dissociate in public because it left me so vulnerable. But at times it was an effective tool, and I was reluctant to let it go altogether. When I was home and experiencing panic, it helped me escape from the severe pain brought up by memories of abuse.

I tried to make myself feel numb to ease the pain and scooted back into the corner with my knees up against my chest. But the pain got worse. It got even harder to breathe. I laid down on my side in a fetal position with my back up against the wall in a familiar way and gave in to Three's demands. I remembered in vivid detail my father pulling me out from under my bed and beating me for hiding from him. I saw all of it in my head and felt most of it in my body. Then I chose to fill my head with cotton so I could gain a little numbness, just enough to dull the pain a bit and cloud the rape scene. I took deep breaths.

David watched me in dismay. Sounding helpless, he asked, "Do you want me to call Dr. Summer?" I could barely hear him. I had given in to Three and was helplessly watching Popi rape me. David picked up the phone and dialed the number he now knew by heart. He sat in the doorway with me while we waited for Dr. Summer to call back. Three knew David, but we were too scared to let him sit close to us. Dr. Summer called back within the hour.

As soon as I heard his voice, I started to sob. I told him about the pain and panic. Dr. Summer calmed me down, then asked, "Is there someone inside that wants to talk to me?" Dr. Summer never talked to parts directly without asking me first. If a part came out and started to talk to him, he responded. But he never reached inside of me to try to identify or speak with a part he suspected was there. That would have felt like a violation. I liked that I and the parts inside had control over whether Dr. Summer talked to them.

"Yes," I said in a very young voice.

"Who am I speaking with?" Dr. Summer asked carefully.

"Olguita, I'm Three." I felt pain in my body that reminded me of what Popi did to me. "Dr. Summer, I feel pain."

"Why are you causing the body pain?"

"Because she needs to know what he did to her."

"Who?"

"Popi."

"She knows what Popi did to her. You've met me in my office before. Do you remember me?"

"Yes, but you don't know all that he did to me and to Mame. She doesn't want to know, and I'm tired of holding it on my own."

"Is that why you're giving Olga pain?"

"Yes. She needs to know what it felt like—how terrible he was."

"Why does she need to know about the pain?"

"It's the only way to get her attention. I know about lots of rapes Popi did that she doesn't want to know about. It could happen again."

"How could it happen again?"

"David could do it."

Dr. Summer paused, then asked, "Would David do that?"

I looked at David and felt Three looking at him. He looked sad. It made me sad to see him like that. Three said, "No. He takes care of us."

"Okay, you wanted me to let Olga know that Popi raped you and your mom a lot and that it hurt. We both know that now, right Olga?"

"Yes, I do," I said wearily.

"Olguita, you're supposed to wait until we have a session to come out. Why are you coming out now?"

"Because there's a lot to know and there are a lot of us inside and we can't wait anymore. We have to make sure she stays safe."

"Olga keeps herself safe. Can you go back to your container until our next face-to-face session on Friday?"

"Yes. If you promise to let us talk next time."

"If Olga wants you to talk at our next session, then you can. Olga, you'll let Three have time at our next session, won't you?"

"Yes," I said in resignation. I knew I couldn't ignore Three. I was exhausted. I cried at the thought of Popi raping me in my bedroom. David's eyes filled with tears as he sat there on the hall floor. Before all of this happened, we'd been having one of the nicest evenings we'd had in a while.

"Olga," Dr. Summer said, "are you feeling better yet?"

"Yes."

"I think we should add another session to our week. Clearly there is too much pressure inside, and three times a week isn't relieving it. I think if parts know they have more time, they may be able to wait for our sessions. I can open up a time on Wednesdays." Opening up a time on Wednesdays was a big deal; that was Dr. Summer's administrative day. "Would that work for you?"

"Sure. I'll have to let work know and I may need another letter to adjust my hours under the ADA, but otherwise yes, it should work."

After I hung up, I hugged David and thanked him for his help. "I'm sorry this is so hard, David." I paused. He never said that it was hard on him, but I could see the worry on his face. I asked, "Could you finish up dinner?" He nodded and I lay down on the sofa, thinking, *I have parts. I have DID. I have to figure out how to live with this better.* My thoughts went back and forth between 1964 and the present. I cried quietly as David finished dinner. We ate in the living room, neither of us talking.

● ○ ●

The next day, Wednesday, I went in for my newly added appointment. Dr. Summer walked me to his office and offered me a cup of tea. I said, "Yes, please."

"Okay, I'll be right back. In the meantime, have a seat." As I sat in my usual chair, I felt small and noticed that all of a sudden I was thinking in Spanish. I felt pain and recognized it as the pain of the rapes. The pain was periodic, not constant, but very sharp. Three was here. She came forward and I could feel myself slump in the chair. When Dr. Summer arrived with the two teas, I set mine down and announced, "I'm here," in a small voice.

Dr. Summer asked, "How are you today?" Since Three had started the conversation, he talked with her directly.

"Better."

"What made things better?"

"You called, you listened, and she listened."

"By 'she' do you mean Olga?"

"Yes."

"So you needed us to know that Popi raped you, is that right?"

"Yes."

"Is there anything else you need us to know?"

"He raped me a lot and it hurt a lot. He made it hurt a lot on purpose. He said mean things to me. He said it was my fault."

"I'm sorry he did that to you, and I'm sorry he said it was your fault. It is important that you know it was *not* your fault. You are just three. He was a grown man and hurt you because *he* wanted to, not because you wanted this. Do you understand?"

I could feel myself hanging on to his words: "It was *not* your fault."

"Did you want Popi to rape you?"

"No."

"Can you feel how it was not your fault?"

"Yes."

"Even if you went to him and started the abuse, it's still not your fault."

I felt my chest tighten and my head spin. I shifted from Three to a part that was five years old. I was still thinking in Spanish. In my mind, I saw myself as a little girl, my hair longer now and with a barrette on my head. I was wearing a plaid shirt. *How did he know I went to Popi and started it? Popi always said, "See, this is your fault. You make me do this to you." How could it not be my fault?* Dr. Summer noticed a subtle change in me.

"Is there another part present?"

"Yes," I said in a small voice. I noticed I was slumped and sat up more. I looked around. Everything seemed new and different. "I like the colors on the walls."

"Thank you. Hi. Who are you?"

"I'm Five."

"Why are you here?"

My head started spinning again. I was overwhelmed by shame. I was silent. *I can't say it. I started it. I went to him. It was my fault. I can't*

172

say it. I felt light-headed. I was starting to get a headache. Three was more present again. There was conflict between Five and Three. Inside, Three said, *He knows it's not our fault. He knows. It's okay to tell him. I can tell him.* Five blurted out, "I went to him. I started it. It was my fault." My head began spinning and I was overwhelmed with shame. I was becoming numb when Dr. Summer started to talk. I focused on him to help me not go away in my head.

He said, "I know. Many children who are abused for a long time learn to start the abuse they know will happen anyway. It's a smart coping strategy. It helped you have some control in an unpredictable, chaotic home."

I nodded. I still felt both Five and Three close to the surface. Five spoke again: "I would go to Popi when I got home from kindergarten if I could hear him upstairs and no one else was home. My chest felt like someone big was sitting on it. My head started spinning and I felt like I was going to jump out of my skin. Then I felt light-headed and another part would take me by the hand and we would go find Popi and start doing what he wanted so he wouldn't hurt us so much. There were other parts of me that would help. We'd look at his face and know what to do. Afterward, Popi would yell at us, 'I told you it was all your fault. You do this to me!' I believed him. But I was too scared to wait until he decided to hurt me. I had to get it over with."

"Can you see how it wasn't your fault?"

I nodded, but I wasn't sure that Five or Three believed him.

"You were trying to survive in a home where you were hurt all the time. It helps to think it's your fault because then you think you can stop it. But you couldn't stop it, could you?"

"No," I said, crying.

"Is Three still there with Five?"

"Yes."

"Are you okay if we use hypnosis to have the parts go into containers?"

"They won't stay in there."

"Okay, but that can be disruptive to Olga's life. How about we have parts go into therapeutic sleep between sessions? They only have to wait two days until Friday. How does that sound?"

"Okay, just until Friday." I took a deep breath. "Ready."

Dr. Summer said, "Close," which had become his shorthand for "Close your eyes." During those months, Dr. Summer used hypnosis to help me have parts come forward and share information, allowing me to learn about the violence from a distance so I didn't have to dissociate. There was a routine to the hypnosis, and I eventually learned to do it myself.

Dr. Summer started with the word "Close." With that, I took a deep breath, closed my eyes, and relaxed into a hypnotic state that was numbing, deep, and calm, but in which my mind wasn't clouded and I wouldn't forget or lose track of what happened. I was able to be there with the parts. Then he would let me know he was going to slowly count to ten. Between one and five, the parts that wanted to could gather and share information with the mind. While he counted from five to ten, any parts that wanted to could become part of the whole, part of Olga. Then he would ask the parts that didn't join the whole to find a container for the memories they held—and for themselves, if they wanted to go into it. Finally, to any parts that didn't like the idea of containers, he offered therapeutic sleep in a comfortable place. Most parts chose this last option. Dr. Summer always brought me back to the present by counting from three to one and saying, "Open."

After he said, "Close," that day, parts gathered and shared information with me. I heard them and took it all in. Three shared more information than I had learned the night before. I saw my bedroom and all the ways my father raped me in there. I also saw my parents' bedroom, the bathroom, and all the other places in our house where my father raped me. I briefly felt the pain of the rapes. As Dr. Summer counted the parts into containers or therapeutic sleep, I felt a little relief.

After that session, I spent a few hours in my usual alcove, waiting to feel strong enough to go home. Dr. Summer checked in with me between sessions. What I was learning from the parts was devastating. I felt raw and vulnerable. I called both David and my office and let them know I'd be going home. I wanted to give up. When David came home, I didn't have the energy to tell him about my session.

David was worrying about the cost of so many sessions. We had the money in savings, but we were going through it quickly. Whenever he expressed this concern to me, I thought it was simple: We had the money and I needed the help. But it wasn't that simple to David. We had worked hard to save. Is this what we wanted to spend it on? Every time we had this discussion, I (and parts inside) started to doubt David. It wasn't unreasonable to have this conversation or feel the way David felt. But I couldn't see that then and often thought, *He doesn't really love me. He loves his money more. When it comes down to it, he will choose his money. I can't trust him. He's going to leave me.*

• • •

I walked into Dr. Summer's office while he was getting two cups of tea and sat in the smaller chair, as had become my custom. I felt sore and tired as usual, my fibromyalgia so constantly with me that I rarely remarked on it anymore. Fibromyalgia gave me a chronic ache near my joints that could get so bad that my skin was painful to the touch. I'd had that kind of pain as long as I could remember, but it had become much worse lately. Suddenly the conversation with the rheumatologist so long ago came back to me. I remember him saying that fibromyalgia was caused by not being able to reach a deep level of sleep, and until that moment in Dr. Summer's office, I hadn't been able to connect that explanation to my experience. I had been sleeping so poorly again, plagued by nightmares and waking up in a sweaty panic.

I could always tell the constant pain of fibromyalgia from the acute pain of memory. Memory pain came with mental pictures of a particular attack and felt like the pain of being raped, sodomized, or kicked in the abdomen and back. It was sharp and didn't stay with me long. The memory of how I felt after abuse—like I had been beaten up—was harder to differentiate from the fibromyalgia, but that pain also came to me with flashbacks, such as images of cleaning myself up.

When Dr. Summer arrived, he handed me one cup of tea and sat down with the other. The brightly colored walls of his office always made me feel a little lighter. I set my cup on the table between the two chairs. There was just enough room for it among a clock, a lamp, and a box of tissues. Dr. Summer had clocks all over his office so he could keep track of time. There were also many boxes of tissues, which I had once found funny and teased him about. But these days, I went through at least one box per session. Dr. Summer was usually in a good mood. Despite dealing with painful and horrible tales of abuse, he seemed to maintain a sincere pleasantness, and I felt like he was always happy to see me. "How are you this morning?" he asked as he sipped his tea.

My relaxed musings stopped, I hurt all over, and my mind instantly started racing uncontrollably: *I see pictures of people hurting me all the time. It's part of the pain. I can't sleep for more than three hours without waking up in a cold sweat. I don't feel like doing anything most of the time. I have to drag myself out of bed. I feel like I'm going through the motions at work and at home with David. I feel burdened by everything. I hate everyone. I feel obsessed with the idea of closing my eyes and never waking up. Popi raped me. He did it a lot. He showed Alex and Mike how to rape me. They showed their friends. Everyone hurt me. Anyone can hurt me. Make this stop!*

I could see Dr. Summer watching me. I wanted to answer him but I couldn't. I couldn't hold on to any of the thoughts long enough to say them. They filled my head, and the more I tried to stop them, the more tired I felt. My eyes felt very heavy and I had to work hard to keep them open.

"It seems to me that you have a lot going on inside. Is that true?"

"Yes," I said, trying to think clearly.

I focused on the thoughts. Finally I was able to hold on to one long enough to tell it to Dr. Summer. I squeezed out, "I have at least one part that watches me while I sleep, and I think that's why I have fibromyalgia." I thought about what I'd just said and wondered how I knew that.

Dr. Summer nodded. "That makes sense."

"Popi showed Alex and Mike what to do to me," I said so softly that Dr. Summer could barely hear. He leaned forward to listen and I shrank down in my chair.

I couldn't look at him. This was really scary to talk about.

He asked, "Is there someone new here?"

"Yes," I said in a teenage voice. I searched around for who this was. The thought popped up that I was Twelve, speaking for a group of parts whose job it was to protect me. "We learned," I said in that same voice, "that we can't trust anyone. We can't even trust her. Lots of us stay up and watch to protect her. We also put up a wall around her when we see people who may try to hurt her."

"I understand that you would not trust. Everyone who was supposed to protect you hurt you. How could you trust?" I felt myself relax a bit. *He understands. Popi, Alex, and Mike raped me, then Mike and Alex with their friends.* I sat silently as these thoughts went through my mind.

"So, who are you protecting?"

"We are protecting Three and the others from Popi. He came to their bedroom at night and made them do things they didn't want to do. And he did things to them that hurt. He also said mean things to them."

"How did you all protect Three and the others?"

"Some protective parts would do certain things so that Three and others didn't have to. They would take turns being there, to make sure the others weren't hurt."

"How would they do that?"

"They would look at Popi's face, the way he walked, and how he sounded and figure out what he wanted. They would listen for him to come in the middle of the night. There were parts that knew just what to say to him, knew just what to do to keep from being hurt too badly. They stayed in the background to watch him because he could change, and then another part needed to come up and do something different."

"Why are you watching Olga sleep now?"

"To make sure she's safe."

"But she's big now. She has David in her life, and he hasn't hurt her. Popi is dead. He can't hurt her anymore."

"Mike and Alex can hurt us."

"I know they hurt you when you were young and after Popi died. But can they really hurt you now? Would David let them hurt you? Isn't Olga smart enough to stop them? She is a lawyer. Don't you think she could protect herself?"

My thoughts went to the present to consider this, then back to the past. I kept going back and forth to figure out if what I was hearing was true. Finally, that young voice responded, "She is smart and strong, but she still needs us to watch over her."

"Why?"

"Because there are others who can hurt her, too."

"Who?"

"You could hurt her."

"That's true, I could." He paused. "But have I ever hurt her?"

"No." I heard my voice get a little quieter. I felt ashamed for saying he could hurt me.

"Have I had opportunities to hurt her?"

"Yes." I, the central me, understood his point.

"If you protect her from everyone, you might keep her safe, but she'll never feel close to anyone. She'll never feel joy. She'll never feel loved the way she should."

I sat silently and my thoughts flew: *How do we stop doing this? This is all we know. But we want to feel close. We want to feel loved more.* I stared at the floor-to-ceiling bookcases just behind Dr. Summer. I tried to make out the titles, but a thought inside tried to refocus me. *Not now.*

I struggled against it. *I want to think about something else. I don't want to tell him. It's too hard.*

If you don't tell him, you'll stay right here in all this pain. He can help you. We can trust him. You already went through the pain. Now you get to tell.

I struggled through the thoughts and the shame. I was afraid to recall this painful memory and say it aloud because if I told Dr. Summer it became real. "After Popi died..." I began to cry and quickly a shift happened. Now I felt like a teenager, but without emotion or fear. I stopped crying. "After Popi died, Alex and Mike hurt me. They tricked me and they showed their friends how to hurt me. They raped me with their friends." My voice was flat as I numbly told him about the gang rapes.

"How do you feel, Olga?"

"Numb and foggy." Mike and Alex had said they'd kill me if I told anyone.

"Let's see if you can come back."

"I don't want to. I don't want to feel this."

"We'll use hypnosis. I don't think dissociation serves you well now. We need you to be able to feel and be alert enough to protect yourself." I reluctantly agreed. He continued, "This is a memory from a long time ago. You are older now. You are a lawyer at the Department of Justice and you are married to David. You are safe now. Can you hear me?"

"Yes," I said, still numb but with a little less cotton in my head.

"Olga, listen to my voice. Can you hear me?"

"Yes." His voice was lifting the dissociation. Panic and pain started to rush in. I began crying uncontrollably.

"Olga, listen to my voice," Dr. Summer said calmly, in a way that was strong but not harsh and got my attention. "Take a deep breath." I did so. "You are big now. Can you see how big you are?" I looked up and down my body. It looked bigger than I thought it should be. I was also surprised that I was dressed in grown-up clothing. I was still crying, but not as hard.

Dr. Summer started the hypnotic process: "Close."

I closed my eyes, took a deep breath, and let go. I felt like I was falling into a hole, but it felt good. "Okay, with one foot here in the present, let's look at what you remembered from the past. As we look at this memory, keep in mind that this happened to you a long time ago. So keep the older you here as you let the younger you come forward. I'm sitting right here next to you. You are safe."

I could feel a change in my thoughts. A younger part came forward and, in Spanish, let me know that she was Eight and that she hadn't felt safe enough to be here until now. I could tell that I was grown up and sitting in Dr. Summer's office, but at the same time I felt young and my body felt small. In this way, an older me and a younger me could be present together, and the older me could comfort the younger me as the memory came up. I described this to Dr. Summer and asked, "Does that make sense?"

"Yes. What do you see?"

"I see Popi at the doorway of my room at night with Alex and Mike. He brings them in and shows them what to do to me." I could see the rest of it but couldn't say it out loud. That would make it too real.

"What else do you see?" I was silent, watching in my head what Eight was showing me. Dr. Summer waited a while before asking, "Are you in your bedroom?"

"Yes."

"What do you see?"

"The ceiling."

"Okay, that's good. What else?"

"The shelves in my room."

"Good. Keep going. Tell me anything you see in your room."

Dr. Summer knew that I didn't want to describe what was terrifying me, but that if I was able to eventually talk about it, the memory would lose its power. So he didn't push too hard. He just asked me to describe generally what I saw, and I slowly got closer to what terrified me.

"I see the window to the bathroom. I see the rosary on my bed."

"Good. Is there anyone in your room?"

"Yes! They are hurting me badly. Popi is showing them how to hurt me. Alex looks evil." My thoughts started to race with all that I had captured in my mind the nights Popi brought Alex and Mike into my room. "I saw their faces. Then blackness."

"Why blackness?"

"I closed my eyes when I saw the looks on their faces." I was having trouble catching my breath. I was wheezing, then sobbing. Dr. Summer reminded the parts that we were big now and this was all a memory. He asked the older me to soothe the younger parts of me that had come forward to tell what they had seen.

Focus. Focus. There in the darkness were Twelve, Eight, Seven, and Five. They were crying. They were scared.

In my mind, I moved closer to them. I tried to soothe them, as Dr. Summer suggested.

They were so small and so scared.

I started crying. *How could Popi hurt me so badly? How could Alex and Mike hurt me?*

Seven said, *Popi made them.* Five showed me Alex's face. Eight said, *No one made him hurt me. He liked it.* Seven reminded all the parts how much Popi beat my brothers and said, *They had no choice.* But Five said, *Alex was always mean and scary.*

I listened from a distance and couldn't embrace the parts or the information they were providing. I wouldn't go any closer. "I'm scared of you," I whispered.

Dr. Summer heard me and asked, "Are you able to soothe the younger parts?"

"No. I'm afraid of what they know!"

Some of the parts pleaded with me. *Won't you hug us? We need to know we're okay. Won't you help us?*

Although I could now acknowledge that the parts were inside me, I was still terrified of getting close to them. The fact that I could feel both young and old at the same time must mean that I had parts, but I vacillated between accepting them and pretending they didn't exist. Likewise, I accepted the DID diagnosis but didn't want to think about having parts and how they were the reason why I was still alive.

"Dr. Summer, I can't. They won't calm down."

He drew me deeper into the hypnosis and said, "Can older parts inside help calm the younger parts that bravely came forward to tell what they saw?" I felt another part of me come closer to my consciousness. She let me know that she was sixteen years old and said she could soothe the younger parts. I thanked her.

After the parts calmed, I felt exhausted. Then the realization that this had happened to *me* settled in. I started to cry. *Dear God, please make this stop! Please make this stop. I want to die.*

Dr. Summer looked both concerned and reassuring. "You're doing good work. We'll need to stop soon. Would you like to stay in the waiting room to see if I have an opening later today? We may be able to finish up this memory and not leave it to torment you." I could feel myself wanting to give up in a profound way, but I couldn't tell if it was a "here and now" feeling, caused by what I was experiencing in the present, rather than events of the past.

We ended the session in our routine way, gathering all the parts that had come forward. I gently helped Five, Seven, Eight, and Twelve into their containers, along with their black plastic trash bags containing all their memories, pictures, feelings, and emotions. I saw myself at age eight closing the lid and then locking the chains.

Afterward, Dr. Summer escorted me to my chair in the alcove. After a while, I called David and work. I was exhausted and was thinking of ways to die. I felt resigned, like I wanted to completely give up trying to lead a regular life. That day Dr. Summer checked in with me between appointments but didn't have a cancellation, so I was there all day. At the end of the day, he came to get me. "I'm worried about you. You look different. Are you are thinking you can't do this anymore?"

I nodded. "I've learned so much and met so many parts already. Do I have to keep going and remember everything? I just don't think I can survive it."

"You already survived it, Olga. Now you're reconnecting your past with your present. Let's go into my office." I got up slowly and could feel pain all over my body. It wasn't the fibromyalgia because it was consistent with the feelings of being raped. I sat down and looked at Dr. Summer, sighing heavily. The pain continued, and the thoughts of dying were growing.

"I have pain, Dr. Summer. It feels old. It feels like what happened."

He nodded. "Can you tell if these feelings are coming from new parts or that same part?"

"Earlier today, I interacted with four parts: Twelve, Five, Seven, and Eight. But the parts giving me these feelings feel different to me."

"How is that?"

"These parts feel angry. I hate Alex and Popi. There's also a part that prays to God to make it all stop and to let us die."

Dr. Summer looked at me with concern on his face. He also looked tired. "I've had a long day, but I don't want to let you go without working through this to give you some peace until our next session."

"Dr. Summer, I can't anymore. I'm tired of trying. I'm tired of getting up in the morning. I'm tired of worrying about David not being able to take this. I'm tired of worrying about losing my job. I'm tired of trying." I was sobbing. I begged, "Please put me in a hospital where this is all I do. Please put me in a hospital where I can sleep. I can't try anymore, Dr. Summer."

"I know you feel like that now, Olga, but it will get better. I know the work you're doing is hard. It's the most painful work a person can do. You're doing the work even though you don't think you are. I know you don't feel like it's getting better, but you've come a long way. I don't think a hospital is the way to go, Olga. I think the structure of your job and the support that you have there, and from David and your friends, is important. I'm afraid that if you're hospitalized now, you won't be able to return to work. You won't have the support you have now. And in the hospital, I wouldn't be able to work with you."

I didn't care. I was exhausted and just wanted to sleep. The hospital seemed like a place I could sleep. "I can't keep doing this."

"Okay, I hear you. What if we make a deal to try something different for six months? After that, if you still want to be admitted into a hospital, I'll help you do that."

"What could we do differently? What would we try?"

"What if I cleared a double session for you every day—Monday through Friday. Right now, you're coming four days a week for a single session, and that doesn't seem to be enough. Your parts are very present and it's making life very hard. Let's see if five double sessions a week would help. Then, on Saturdays, you can see the art therapist here. She's very good. I'll see if she can make time for you. On Sundays, you can call to check in with me if you want. I can also prescribe an antidepressant to help even out your mood and an anti-anxiety medication, Klonopin."

I felt confused. "Why an antianxiety medication?"

"When parts come forward, they cloud your mind with emotions from the past and body memories. Having your mind become cloudy causes you anxiety. Then the added memories, pain, or emotions heighten that anxiety. I think the Klonopin will help with that, and it will probably help you sleep better. It should help with the panic attacks too, but you need to learn to catch these early or you'll have to take a lot, which may affect your ability to work."

"Okay, six months."

"Yes, and remember that you can always call when you need to. Don't wait for your sessions."

I went home that night and collapsed onto the couch. I was too tired to talk to David, and I was afraid to tell him about the deal Dr. Summer and I had made.

When I filled him in the next morning, David was worried. He agreed that working and staying home instead of going to a hospital was a good idea, but our insurance only covered fifty visits a year, and I was already way over that amount. David had seen about a third of our savings go to my appointments and suggested that I ask Dr. Summer if we could pay a set amount each month so that later, when I started seeing him less often, the amount would balance out and cover his fees from before.

I could see how much David worried about having savings for when we needed it, but to me this was a time when we needed it. "I can borrow from my retirement account if this is going to be a problem for you, David. But I don't feel I can ask Dr. Summer to take less money now and pay him more later. We have the money and I think we should pay him his full fees. I don't want this to affect my working relationship with him."

David reluctantly agreed to dip further into our savings, but I think he resented it. In that moment, my mistrust of David grew. I feared that money was more important to him than me and my needs. I never shook that feeling.

I went to Dr. Summer's office the next morning and began the deal: daily double sessions and medication.

Choosing Not to Run

12

I nervously waited for my boss, Rosie, whose meeting was running late. I needed yet another change in my schedule, this time to see Dr. Summer every day. Rosie didn't normally make me this nervous. She was the assistant attorney general of the Office of Justice Programs, the part of the Department of Justice that distributed grants. I had been working at the office for four years now and was the lead lawyer, or general counsel, and we were in the middle of implementing the Violence Against Women Act. It was groundbreaking legislation. New laws strengthened how communities could support victims of sexual assault, stalking, and domestic violence. Special provisions offered remedies to immigrant women who were being abused by their husbands. This work felt indescribably important to me, especially now, as I was uncovering memories of abuse.

Rosie and I worked closely together and she was easy to talk to. When I first told her I was a survivor of childhood sexual abuse, she was very supportive and empathetic, accepting my need to attend therapy sessions twice a week and encouraging me to do whatever I needed to get through this. We had appointed my deputy, Peter, to be her main contact when I was out of the office and unavailable, and that seemed to be working well. But now that Dr. Summer and I had this new agreement, I needed to meet with Rosie yet again before I submitted the paperwork that adjusted my accommodation under the Americans with Disabilities Act. I knew that according to the ADA my request had to be honored, but she didn't have to keep me in the same position, as general counsel.

I waited and worried. I was nervous about telling Rosie that I was now going to therapy sessions every day. I'd worked so hard to get to this place in my life, and I didn't want to lose it. The healing process was more demanding than I could ever have imagined. The toll it was taking on me must have been obvious. My usual smile was gone. I cried a lot. I'd lost so much weight that I looked sick, and my face was pale, with dark circles under my eyes. I didn't realize how I looked until friends at work started noticing the changes. Some people knew I was dealing with memories of being abused as a child, but others whom I didn't know as well just saw changes in me and expressed their concern.

When I finally got to meet with Rosie this time, things felt different right away. She greeted me without her usual warmth and stood behind her desk rather than coming around to the couch, where we usually sat together. She seemed distracted and it unnerved me. *She's upset with us. She doesn't want me in my job anymore. I can't trust her.* Sadness and disappointment overtook me. Suddenly her office felt very big. Her enormous desk felt even larger than normal, and the leather chairs felt unwelcoming. *Something is happening. This isn't good.* I fought the feeling of panic.

In my work with Dr. Summer, I had learned that a good way to manage anxiety and stress was to focus on one thing at a time. For example, I started breaking my schedule down into manageable increments. Although I was ambitious, always planning and thinking ahead to future career goals, I let all of that go. When suicide is constantly with you, as it was with me at that time, surviving is all that matters. I broke time down into the smallest increments and focused on what was in front of me in each moment. Thinking too far ahead overwhelmed me and the feelings of wanting to die would come up strongly. That day with Rosie, I pushed aside the constant fears about losing everything—my job, my marriage, my friends—and focused on getting through the conversation, ignoring everything else. I told myself I would deal with the other stuff later.

I hesitantly started to let her know about the changes I needed to make in my schedule. Rosie looked concerned. I wasn't sure if it was concern over how I was doing personally or concern about how she was going to accomplish everything with a general counsel who wasn't doing well. I put that thought out of my head and forged on: "Rosie, I want to let you know that I'm submitting a change to my ADA schedule. I'm starting to see my psychiatrist every day for ninety minutes. I'll do what I'm doing now, keeping some core hours at the office, but I may need to work more from home. But I will either work my required hours or submit for leave."

"Have you talked to Marty about this?" Marty was the head of administrative services, which included personnel.

"Not yet. I wanted to talk to you first. I know it's already hard for you to reach me. Do you have any concerns about this change?"

"I can still reach Peter when you're gone, so I think it should be okay. I think you should talk to Marty and work out what he needs from you. I want you to have whatever support you need. If you need more sessions, then you should have the flexibility for more sessions." Part of me protested, *Her actions don't match her words.* Doubt was building up inside me.

"Rosie, do you want me to move out of the general counsel position? I can if you need me to. We could find another position for me. The ADA doesn't require you to keep me in the same job. It just requires that I not lose any salary or benefits due to the disability." Although I tried to stay calm, my heart was pounding and my thoughts were racing as I brought this up. *She seems cold. She's afraid of us. She doesn't want us anymore. Protect yourself.* I had learned in my sessions with Dr. Summer that at least one part of me had the role of looking for inconsistencies in other people. The distrust would grow until I no longer felt safe around certain people. If I had to be around one of these people, at work for example, a big wall would come up and the person would become almost two-dimensional. All I could see was that I couldn't trust the person.

Through the rushing of blood in my ears and the pounding in my chest I heard Rosie say, "No, don't be silly. Just go talk to Marty." Watching her closely, I doubted her honesty even more. I started feeling that numb sensation in my head. Inside I could hear older parts soothing younger parts. *It'll be okay. Just get through this meeting. We'll figure it out. We'll need to stay away from her and we can do that. Don't worry, she's not Popi or Mame.*

I left Rosie's office with a sense of impending doom. My thoughts were still racing and the numbness was getting worse. I found Marty in his office right away. He was on the phone but warmly waved me in. When his call was over, he came around to the other side of his desk to sit next to me. I searched his eyes and saw kindness and concern. Marty and I worked together regularly and got along well. He asked what I needed, and I explained to him about the change in my work schedule. He told me that Rosie had been concerned about my frequent absences and was considering having me move into another position. My thoughts raced again. *See, I told you. She lied. She can't be trusted. Stay away from her.* The rushing of blood was pounding in my ears. *This is Marty. He tells you the truth. Calm down. It's okay. We can work with Marty.*

I took a deep breath and heard Marty say that Rosie didn't want to hurt me. "She'll create a position for you that will allow you to go to your appointments and still have a job that feels meaningful. You'll have your same pay and benefits." I was calmer. *We'll work something out. We're not going to work for Rosie. We can't trust her. We'll go somewhere else.*

"Thanks for telling me, Marty. I appreciate your honesty. Can I be the one to figure out what position to move into?" He agreed and told me he would let Rosie know. I gave him the letter Dr. Summer wrote justifying my accommodation and left his office before he had a chance to read it. I told him I would email him about a new position in a day or two.

I knew exactly where I wanted to go: the Office for Victims of Crime (OVC). As general counsel, I had worked with its director, Veronica, and had come to respect and admire her. The more I learned about the abuse I'd survived, the more I wanted to let the world know that it happens and help other victims of abuse as best I could. It was ironic that I was in a position to help even before I knew what had happened to me. My ambitions were changing. I cared less about reaching a certain level of status. Making a difference in people's lives was beginning to be more important. If I couldn't work on implementing the Violence Against Women Act, I believed that working for OVC might give me more influence on issues related to child abuse, domestic violence, and sexual assault.

Before her current appointment, Veronica had worked directly with sexual assault survivors. I stopped by her office, feeling much more self-assured. I had something to offer her if she wanted it. I said, "Veronica, would you be interested in having me come to work for you? I would bring a funded position, so you wouldn't have to give up one of yours. I could be your legal counsel."

She was keenly interested but curious about why Rosie would be willing to transfer a position from the general counsel's office to her office. Then she asked, "Olga, why would Rosie let you go?" A fear rose up in me, along with a flood of conflicting thoughts: *Tell her. No, don't tell her. She has to know. She doesn't have to know everything. Will she want us?*

I took a deep breath and, fighting back tears, asked her if I could sit down. She said, "Yes, please," then looked at me closely and picked up the phone to push back her next appointment. I sat there for a moment trying to collect myself. I didn't want to cry and sound pathetic while asking if I could work for her.

"Veronica, for the past two years I've been recalling memories of abuse from when I was a child. I'm in therapy, but it's a grueling process. I have an ADA accommodation to see my therapist four times a week, but I'm about to start seeing him five times a week for ninety-minute sessions. I'm not able to be there for Rosie when she needs me. General counsel is a demanding position, and I'm not up to it. You don't have a legal counsel, and if you're willing to work with my limitations, I'll ask to be transferred here." I felt breathless.

Veronica came around her desk and sat in the chair next to me. "I would love to have you in my office. You would bring a wealth of knowledge—not just your legal skills, but an understanding of what a victim goes through. You can help us all keep that in mind. You can help us understand healing and trauma. But first, do whatever you need to, with my full support. We'll set you up in an office near mine so you can come and go as you need and have privacy when you're here. Then, as you get better—which you will, Olga…" I had started to cry silently. "You will get better, even if it doesn't feel like it now." She reached out for my hand.

She paused for a moment and then continued, "When you get better, you'll help us develop better programs and better responses and remind us who we work for. So you see, I get a great deal. I get you the lawyer and you the survivor."

After a moment, I collected myself and thanked her. I walked down the five flights of stairs to my office, avoiding the elevator because I didn't want to be seen crying. Back at my office, I was surprised to find Marty waiting for me. He had Dr. Summer's letter in his hand. Dr. Summer had written about how this change in schedule was to address my weakening condition. He had outlined how I was unable to eat, that my sleep was disturbed, and that I was having increasing suicidal feelings stemming from major depression. He also said that as a result of childhood abuse, I had post-traumatic stress disorder, panic and anxiety disorders, and dissociative identity disorder. Finally, the letter said that he hoped this accommodation would allow me to keep working in a supportive environment and avoid being hospitalized. Marty's eyes were red.

He said, "I'm so sorry. I'm not sure we've been the supportive workplace you thought we were. I'll help you in whatever way I can." Crying again now myself, I closed the door and hugged him.

"Thank you. You're a good friend." We sat there with tears streaming down our faces. "Marty, I want to go to OVC as Veronica's legal counsel. I just talked to her and she likes the idea. Can you make it happen?" He nodded. I paused and then told him what I'd been worrying about for months: "I'm afraid that people will find out about my diagnosis and that I might lose my security clearance." I felt so vulnerable telling him.

"Does Veronica know all this?" He held up the letter.

"No, I didn't tell her that much."

"I won't show it to anyone. I'll just tell Rosie that I have what I need to justify the accommodation."

I thanked him, trying not to start crying again. I gave him another hug, and he left to make the necessary arrangements with Veronica and Rosie. As I sat at my desk, it occurred to me that this was why Dr. Summer wanted me to keep working. I thought of Marty's kindness, Veronica's overwhelming support, and even Rosie's flexibility about my therapy appointments. In the midst of everything I was going through, it was very powerful. *Marty knows I have DID and he doesn't act like I'm crazy.* He didn't treat me with anything but warmth and respect. Veronica had talked about the value I would bring to her office. Rosie, too, would be supportive and approve my move to OVC. Warmth spread through me—something I hadn't felt in a while—providing a little relief from all of the darkness inside.

● ● ●

In sessions with Dr. Summer, I was developing the skills to manage my life when my inside world was divided and full of fear. This involved uncovering more parts, learning what they knew about my past, hearing how they felt, and welcoming them in, or integrating them. In what seemed like a slow and endless process, I gradually gained more insight and knowledge about my life and the triggers that took me back to the past in a panic.

Dr. Summer set a routine for our sessions, and I soon knew what to do and how to do it. Each day I'd come into his office and sit in the smaller chair sipping my tea. Within minutes, my mind would fill with thoughts. It didn't bother me as much as it used to. I learned to let the thoughts wash over me, accepting them and not being so afraid of what I was learning. I would listen closely to my thoughts, tell Dr. Summer what they were, and then tell him which thought or part most urgently needed to be addressed that day. I learned to listen so well by having Dr. Summer listen to me and ask questions. When I reported a thought like "I feel scared today," Dr. Summer would ask, "Who is it that's scared?" Then I'd search around in my head, asking, *Who is scared?* A thought would come up and I'd answer: "Five is scared." Then Dr. Summer would ask why. By the end of that session, Dr. Summer, Five, and I would have had a detailed conversation about what Five was feeling and how I could help. Then we would orient Five to the present and to me as an adult.

I was now checking in with parts automatically. If one part felt particularly close to the surface, I'd suggest we talk about what she was remembering. If more than one indicated an urgency, I'd sit silently and mediate which memory would come out first and try to make time for both in that session.

I felt more in control of what we talked about. The parts were starting to trust Dr. Summer and me. My sessions were more productive, but despite my signs of progress, I hated the process. It was so painful remembering the attacks. I couldn't get away from the thoughts, scenes of abuse, and emotions that I had hidden from myself for so long. Even though meeting my parts helped me manage my life better and heal, the process was also devastating.

As I sat in Dr. Summer's office, I felt like I was back in my family's home being attacked. I cried so hard I couldn't breathe. I got intense headaches from crying and from parts that held the pain of what had been done to me. Giving in to the despair allowed other parts to come up and share the pain of the attacks. I felt pain inside me from the rapes, and I felt pain all over from being beaten and tensing my body during the attacks. Part after part had held the pain away from me when I was experiencing the abuse, and even now I felt like remembering the experience would kill me. Most of the time I *wished* it would kill me.

"Dr. Summer," I cried, "this hurts so much! I can't bear this much pain." I pleaded with him to make it go away.

"You have already survived this pain, Olga," he said softly, as he had told me so many times before. I focused on his words, trying to believe that if I was strong enough to survive it as a child, I could survive the remembering now. "I wish I could make it stop, but you know I can't. As you go through this process, you'll see that the dissociation kept the knowledge, sensation, pain, and emotion away from you. But it left you numb. And it left you without defenses. You're unraveling the dissociation so you can be safe, so your past doesn't control you."

Dr. Summer stayed right with me, reminding me over and over, "This isn't happening today. This only feels like it's happening now. Try to keep a part of you in today as you go back in time." I went through this process with each part. Despair would come first, pulling me into a dark hole and then growing until I was on the edge of losing myself in the darkness. *I have no family. They attacked me like I was a thing, an animal they could do anything to. They didn't treat me like a daughter or a younger sister. I had no father. I had no brothers.* Then I would give in and stop fighting what my body was trying to show me. It was overwhelmingly painful that Popi, Mike, and Alex raped me. They raped me so often and so viciously that I'd wanted to die. I prayed for it, wished it with every ounce of my being, and in that way created parts to commit suicide. *I had no one. I was all alone in a crazy family. I couldn't trust anyone.* Each time I fell into the black hole of despair, I managed to come back out of it alive.

Feeling this deeply was new to me, having dissociated through most of my life to keep all feelings away. Even though most of what I was feeling was emotional and physical distress, I was vaguely aware that Dr. Summer was right: My ability to feel good and to feel joy was also growing. When I was able to hear it, he would encourage my progress by reminding me, "This all feels awful right now, but you'll eventually also feel the good in your life. The deeper the feelings you can access, the deeper of both ends of the spectrum you'll be able to feel—good and bad."

And thanks to David, who had the forethought to make sure we went on vacation each year, I soon had the opportunity to experience the other end of the spectrum. In the midst of my despair, we went to Disney World. It was so much fun. I experienced pure joy at being in a place with cartoon characters walking around, come to life. I could sense parts inside, the younger parts especially, feeling happier than they had ever been. This new level of joy was radically different from the despair just a week before, when I so desperately wanted to die.

My feelings continued to shift wildly like this for a while. All feelings seemed new to me, and very intense. The intermittent joy and happiness, when I could savor them, helped me realize what life could be like. When I felt happy, it was like a drug. It drove me. I wanted more of it, so I kept working on healing, including listening to my parts. As painful as it was, I had to do it. If I ignored them, they would give me even more pain in an effort to get my attention. Dr. Summer helped by being a witness to their stories. In our sessions, parts gathered together, shared all of their memories, and integrated into me. As I integrated parts, I felt relief from the pain. I had more clarity and was less burdened. For a short time afterward, I felt focused and sharp in my thinking. I imagined this was how people who weren't divided felt all the time. I gradually came to realize that the more I integrated, the less emotional and physical pain I experienced. Instead of individual parts having to bear the burden of what happened on their own, the emotions were now spread throughout the whole of me. An unfamiliar sense of calm began to surface.

● ○ ●

I was getting stronger, but the memories were getting worse, like one of those computer games that gets progressively harder to match your increasing skill. My agile mind was still protecting me by keeping memories away until I was strong enough to deal with them. During a session toward the end of the six-month deal I had made with Dr. Summer, a part of me came forward that held only a pair of eyes. I didn't know whose they were or what their significance was. Then another part came forward with more information about the eyes. The eyes were watching Mike and his friend Harold rape me in the bathroom. It still didn't make sense because I already knew that Mike and Harold had raped me. Then another part offered the face that belonged to the eyes. It was my mom's face. I was suddenly flooded with parts that had more information about that memory. My mom saw Mike and his friend rape me in the bathroom when I was eighteen. Her eyes were at first dazed and then disgusted, and then she simply walked away. These details had been kept hidden behind another door within the room that held the original memory of the rape.

Suddenly I felt suicidal. Dr. Summer and I worked hard to identify the part that held the feelings of wanting to die. This suicidal part was supposed to guard that inner room—the one holding the memory that my mom saw it all and walked away. Her betrayal had been devastating. What I learned in that session was that after that rape I opened the medicine cabinet and took whatever pills were in there. I went to my room, crawled into the corner by the bed, and fell asleep only to wake up vomiting in the middle of the night.

These memories rocked me to the core. I was starting to remember that my mom could have stopped my brothers' attacks and for some reason didn't. During this time I also started remembering that my father prostituted me. I remembered him taking me to the houses of men who would rape me in front of him and then pay him. It wasn't until many years later that I recalled my mother's role in my prostitution. I also began to remember that Mike's friends sometimes paid him. The pain of everything I was remembering was unbearable. *I never had a family.*

During those six months, when I wasn't working or in therapy sessions I was sleeping on the couch. I was so afraid of the panic attacks that I avoided anything that might trigger them and simply stopped going places that might overwhelm me. I avoided people whom some of my parts didn't trust. I stopped running in races, working out at the gym, and going to the grocery store and had lost contact with most of my friends.

David was almost always with me. He heard all that I was remembering, and he witnessed and supported me through all the despair and pain. The bags under his eyes and the heaviness in his step showed how grueling the process was for him, as well. The members of David's support group told him he needed to take breaks. He needed to see his friends, think about something else, play golf. He needed to get away from it for just a bit. I knew they were right, but that didn't stop me from getting angry.

He came home from a support group meeting one night and sat down with me on the couch. "I love you, Olga, but I'm tired. Hearing what you learn in your daily sessions is exhausting. I feel like we're surrounded by a morass of darkness and evil." I sighed. I felt like a problem. My thoughts started spinning. *He's going to leave me. He's too tired. It's all too ugly for anyone to hear. He wants to get away from me.* Fear surged in me. I was afraid to be alone.

"What do you want to do, David? Are you going to leave me?" I challenged him, feeling cold inside. It felt like my heart was freezing. Gone were the context of our relationship and any feelings of love toward him. My thoughts turned drastically, but I didn't notice that I was different. *He wants to go have fun without me—take a break from all this. But even when I'm out with my friends, this is all I think about. At work this is all I think about. I can't get away from it. But he can? How is that okay?* I didn't realize at the time that this reaction belonged to the parts whose job it is to not trust others. At the time, it just felt like I was mad. But in these situations, my levels of anger, coldness, and self-righteousness were always off the charts, never matching the situation. That night I was furious but didn't admit it. I agreed that David should have a break and punished him by never telling him about my sessions again.

In my mind, I had already lost David. I believed it strongly. I started leaning on my friends for support again, spending whole weekends away. I would drive to my friend Bonnie's house, eat lunch with her and her husband, watch TV in their family room, and often fall asleep. My friends Sue and Kathleen, whom I had known since elementary school, often met me for lunch or dinner. I told them only that I was remembering that I was sexually abused by my father, and later I told them that my brothers abused me too. Neither was surprised. "I always thought there was something weird about your family," Kathleen remarked. It was a relief to hear her say that. I couldn't have taken it if my oldest friends didn't believe me.

When I didn't have the energy to go out, Sue and Kathleen would come over and bring food. I felt their warmth and support very strongly. I eventually told them about the DID and they didn't seem afraid of me. They asked questions, which made me feel that they cared a lot.

David and I had been going through this for two and a half years. He was exhausted, I was exhausted, and I had changed toward him. I believed he was going to leave me, and I had to figure out how to not feel the pain of losing him. I felt abandoned and angry when David's worry about our savings came up and when he took care of himself by getting together with friends and playing golf.

My doubts about him grew and the mistrustful parts came closer to the surface. I felt crabby and negative. I no longer trusted him or confided in him. More distance came between us, and I didn't know how to talk about it. In the fall of 1995, I told him I didn't love him anymore, that I only felt sad and cold. The part of me that froze my heart was so entrenched and habitual for me that I didn't notice it was only one part of me. It genuinely felt like me. I couldn't even articulate why I no longer had feelings for David or why things had changed. I asked him for a separation. He didn't argue; he just asked why. I told him I was unhappy.

He packed a few things and went to stay with a friend. Our two cats stayed with me. David believed that we would be able to get back together. But once he was gone, the mistrustful parts calmed down and retreated. The relief I felt at their absence only seemed to confirm that I was doing the right thing. I was starting to feel better. I could take care of myself. I had made it through those six months and was much stronger. My friends were helping me, my office was supportive, and David wasn't who I thought he was. He was someone whose words didn't match his actions.

At the time, neither David nor I recognized what was going on. It took such a long time for anyone to gain my trust, yet they could lose it in a moment, with just a word or an action, without ever knowing it. I lost track of who David really was: the friend I made in law school, the one who taught me how to study, helped me get away from my past, and became my first real family. I lost track of the husband who slept on the living room floor beside me and who sat with me through the night as I cried. I lost my best friend. David and I divorced two years later.

It took us two more years, but eventually David and I managed to be friends. He remained one of the most amazing men I know and

I will always love him. My trust issues were largely responsible for the end of many of my intimate relationships. Only much later would I learn about the mistrustful parts that developed in me when I was very young, finally meet those parts, and try to accept why they were a part of me. They were very good at keeping me safe, but sadly also very good at keeping me from sustaining close intimate relationships—what I wanted most in life.

13

Jan was the grant manager in the Office for Victims of Crime. She had worked there a number of years and was a passionate advocate for victims and the mission of the office. She had strong opinions about how the office should award grants and on which victims we should focus our efforts. Under prior directors, Jan had enjoyed a great deal of influence. But Veronica came to her directorship straight from the victim services field and had her own vision for the office. She didn't rely on Jan's guidance as heavily as the previous director had—a difficult change for Jan, whose passion could get the better of her. Jan often strongly and loudly insisted that a project could or could not be funded. By the time I moved to OVC, I knew Jan from her many trips to the general counsel's office to try to stop Veronica from funding a particular organization. One of my jobs as the new legal counsel in OVC was to determine whether our efforts fell within the Victims of Crime Act. This meant Jan and I now had even more contact than before. It was often very unpleasant.

One day I realized that every time I ran into Jan my head felt fuzzy. If she talked to me, I felt anxious and fuzzier still, like my head was full of cotton. I stopped being able to think clearly.

I'd been dissociating all my life, but this was one of the first times I was able to identify myself doing it outside of Dr. Summer's office. I was so used to feeling fuzzy and calm that it was hard to detect; feeling this way had always been in the way of recognizing that I felt this way. But integrating more parts had started making me more focused and clearheaded. The more I integrated, the sharper my mind felt. I loved this feeling of clarity and wanted more of it.

I walked into my next session with Dr. Summer feeling victorious for simply having noticed that I dissociated when I saw this colleague. As I described the feelings I had when I was around Jan, Dr. Summer confirmed that this was the way I had described dissociation in our sessions, then asked, "Why do you think you dissociate around Jan?"

"I don't know. But I don't like it. I like feeling sharp and clear in my thinking."

Dr. Summer smiled. "It's nice to hear you say that. It is a good feeling, isn't it? It will get even better as you integrate more and figure things out."

I could tell Dr. Summer was proud of my progress, and I paused for a second to hold on to that feeling. It was like making a parent proud. "Dr. Summer, when my thoughts get clouded around Jan, I get anxious and start feeling the panic pain."

"Okay, let's try this: When you're around Jan, pay attention to the dissociation. When you get that fuzzy feeling, stop to notice what happened just before it came up."

"Sometimes it's just that she walked by or that we're in a meeting together. Parts inside are afraid of her. She's loud and always blaming someone for something."

"I see. What is her position in the office?"

"She's a grants manager."

"Is she at a higher level than you?"

"No, I report to the director."

"Can she hurt you, really?"

"No, not really. But it feels like she could."

"Who is it that's afraid of her?"

"Young parts are afraid of her. She yells a lot."

"You need to show the young parts that you can take care of them. When you figure out what happens before the fuzzy feeling, then you will know what to change or stop."

"Okay, I'll try."

After that, I watched my interactions with Jan more carefully. One day, she found me in my office to let me know she disagreed with my legal opinion allowing Veronica to fund a project. The day before, Veronica had come to me with a question about the project. Jan had told her it was illegal, and Veronica wanted to know if I agreed. I researched the issue, conferred with a couple of other attorneys, and concluded that the project was indeed allowable. I recommended that Veronica fund the project and agreed to oversee it if she wanted me to.

Jan came into my office to confront me. In a very loud voice, she said that the project couldn't be done and that I was violating the law. I panicked and dissociated right away. She stood so close and yelled so loud that my ears felt the rushing of blood and I couldn't hear anymore. I noticed that I was outside my body the way I was with Popi. My eyes felt fixed and unfocused. Even so, I paid attention to how I felt. I didn't say a word. I just stood there. Jan stopped yelling, looked at me, and then said she was going to report me and stormed out.

I stood there feeling clouded and unfocused. *She yelled at me.* Then more thoughts came: *That's what she does before I feel this way. She's unpredictable, and that's scary.* To this array of thoughts, Five added, *She also scrunches up her face.* I slowly closed my door, then walked to my desk and sat down. I just stared for a while as the thoughts flew around my head: *I don't know how to stop her. She's scary. What do I do?*

I thought for a little while. Mostly younger parts were present, and they didn't have any ideas about how to handle the situation. Slowly and gently, older parts moved the younger ones out of the way and suggested, *You could keep your office door closed.*

But what if she opens it?

You could tell her not to yell. You could tell her to get out.

All of these suggestions sounded scary to the young parts inside. But I decided to give them a try.

207

The next morning I came into the office early. I made a pot of coffee, settled in at my desk, and pulled out the project file Veronica had given me. I called the grant applicant to let them know their funding had been approved. I kept my door closed. I was waiting for Jan and I was scared, but mostly I felt sharp and clearheaded. I wasn't sure what I would do or say, but I was determined to stand up to her. I had just picked up the phone to make another call when my door opened. I slammed down the phone and jumped out of my chair.

Jan looked angry and was waving a piece of paper at me. In a loud voice, she reiterated that the project I had approved was illegal. *This time I'm going to do it. I'm going to stop her before I start feeling fuzzy.* I walked right up to her and stood very close, intentionally in her space. "Jan, stop! You cannot yell at me for any reason whatsoever. Do you understand me?" She looked shocked. I had never done anything like that before. She lowered her voice but continued to tell me that I was breaking the law.

I firmly said to her in a low, calm voice, "I'm tired of your accusations. You cannot tell me what the law says or doesn't say until you have a law degree." I pointed at the diplomas I had on my wall. "When you have these, you can come and calmly talk to me about your interpretation of the law. Until then, you cannot." Speechless, Jan looked stunned. I continued, "If you're concerned about the grant programs we fund, you can make an appointment with me to discuss your concerns. But you will not burst into my office again, you will not tell me the law, and you will not yell at me, ever. Now please leave."

Jan stood there, staring. I noticed that her stare looked familiar; it reminded me of the way my own face felt sometimes. I felt sad for her. My tone changed, and I asked Jan if she was okay.

"Yes, I'm fine."

"Would you like to make an appointment to talk about your concerns?" I asked, more softly.

She continued to stare but seemed more present, and grateful for the change in my tone. "Yes, please. I'm concerned that the money won't be used properly."

"Okay," I said with a sadness in me. *She's been hurt, too. She looks like us. She's not so scary. She's just scared.* We set up an appointment for that afternoon. Jan left, walking with less confidence. It felt good to take care of myself, but I was sad to realize that this woman whom I had thought of as a threat seemed to have been hurt herself.

When I told Dr. Summer, he was proud of me for stopping her, and also for being able to see the hurt in her. He helped me understand that I protected myself by setting a boundary, and that it worked. "You are showing that you can stop dissociating and take care of yourself. You are also showing compassion for those whose hurt comes out differently." I sat in his office and cried for what I saw in Jan, for the despair and pain I knew she and I both felt.

I continued keeping an eye on when I dissociated and noticing what happened to cause it, and began to take action to stop or prevent those situations. Whenever I felt it, I stopped it as soon as possible. After many months, I more often felt clear and present than dissociative. If someone I didn't know stood too close to me or tried to talk to me on the subway, I moved away. It took time and effort, and sometimes I reverted to dissociating. But I kept working on it.

● ◦ ●

After David moved out, I started doing my grocery shopping at a small market close to where I lived. It was expensive, but I liked it because it was quiet, rarely crowded, and within walking distance. Eventually, after months of eating takeout and buying essentials at the market, I wanted to go to the grocery store to restock the kitchen and get cat food.

One Saturday morning I mustered up the courage to drive to one of the largest grocery stores in the area. When I saw all the cars in the parking lot, I felt a tightening in my chest. I drove round and round and finally found a space at the very far end of the lot. The tightness in my chest got worse. I sat in my car watching the shoppers around me come and go and trying to catch my breath. *People everywhere. How are we going to be safe around all these people? They look mean.* I stepped out of the car and instantly felt pain in my abdomen. "Okay," I said to myself out loud. "I hear you." My thoughts bounced around. *They could hurt us. We can't protect ourselves from all these people.* The parking lot felt chaotic. I sighed, got back in my car, and stopped by the little market on the way home. I felt defeated.

At my next session, I said, "Dr. Summer, I'm having trouble going to the grocery store. When I tried to go this weekend, my chest got tight and I felt pain when I got out of the car. I sat in the car for a while trying to calm down, but the only thing that calmed me was driving home." I was discouraged. There were just so many things I couldn't do anymore. "When is this going to stop, Dr. Summer? I have to be able to go grocery shopping."

"What is behind your disappointment?"

"I want to be able to take care of myself and I have to be able to take care of my cats, but I have a hard time being around a lot of people."

"I see. Okay. We can work on that. But first, let me point out all the progress you've made. Olga, you've been moving along in your therapy incredibly well. You're listening to what's going on inside, learning to notice when you're about to dissociate, and choosing to stay present and be assertive. You can now identify when you're getting overwhelmed before it totally takes over. You bring greater acceptance of parts into our work. You are building trust inside. I'm proud of you, Olga. There is still work to do, but over the past few years you've made extraordinary progress."

I paused to think about what he was saying. I took a deep breath and sat up a bit in my chair. This was something I needed in our work together. Dr. Summer constantly redirected my focus from all that I thought was wrong and helped me see everything I'd accomplished. He did this all the time in my work with him. For some reason, hearing it once was never enough. So he would show me over and over again the ways I was getting better and then challenge me to keep going, to make the next step.

"We need to develop better strategies to help you manage situations that feel chaotic. The way I see it, there are two things going on here. First, we need to strategize how you can take care of yourself: go to the store, ride the metro system, take care of your pets, and generally move through the world without dissociation, pain, or panic. The second thing I hear is that young parts are upset in certain situations, like crowds and overstimulating environments. Does this sound right to you?"

I could feel a change inside me when Dr. Summer said this about younger parts. My thoughts changed quickly. I shrunk back in my chair and a small voice said, "Yes."

"It seems like someone new is here?"

I nodded.

"Is it okay to talk to you?"

I nodded again.

"Are you the one who doesn't like the grocery store?"

"Yes," came the same soft voice.

"What is it about the grocery store?"

"It's not the store; it's the people. We get scared that some big person is going to hurt us. So we don't let her go places where there are lots of people."

I felt dizziness in my head and then a different voice—a little stronger but still young—came out: "And then there's all that noise. We won't let her go in places with too much noise."

"Is there someone new here?"

"Yes."

"Is it okay if we talk together?"

"Yes."

"What's the problem with the noise?"

"It was always noisy. A lot of yelling and crying. There was too much going on."

"Is that the same kind of problem the other part has?"

"Yes. It's too hard for her to watch everyone to figure out who is going to hurt us next."

"Don't you think Olga can take care of you?"

"We want to think that, but we aren't sure."

"Why is that?"

"Because she couldn't take care of us before."

"Do you all know what year it is?"

"1968?"

"Oh, I see. No, it's 1996, and Olga is big now. You all live inside her, and she has learned about you. She is also learning how to stop people from hurting you. She is strong and powerful. Were you there when she stopped the woman in the office from yelling at you?"

"It's 1996? She's big?" I paused to let the information sink in to all the parts that were listening. "She stopped people from yelling at us?"

"Yes." Dr. Summer watched and waited. Home had been so chaotic. I had to watch Popi, Mike, Alex, and my mom very carefully. *But I don't live there anymore. I'm grown up now.* My eyes shifted rapidly from side to side. I felt dizzy, and then I felt a pressure in the center of my forehead. It felt as though my eyes were focused toward the center, inside me. I recognized this feeling. Parts were gathering. They had learned that they didn't need to be separate from me and from each other anymore.

In my own adult voice, I softly let Dr. Summer know, "Parts are gathering."

"Close." In our usual way, Dr. Summer helped parts share information among themselves through hypnosis, and many young parts integrated. When he said, "Open," I opened my eyes and felt clearer and lighter, my mind a little sharper. I felt relaxed and proud of myself.

My thoughts immediately went back to the grocery store. *I need to be able to shop for food. I need to be able to take care of myself.* "Dr. Summer, how do I go to the grocery store?"

"It should be easier now. Try going when there aren't so many people, and then, when you're ready, work up to going at busier times. Also, think of ways to break down the experience into manageable parts, just like we did when you were depressed. Make a grocery list, but don't feel like you have to get everything all at once. Focus hard on the list, and not on all the things going on around you. Pick a store where you're familiar with the aisles and setup. Try this and vary it as you feel inside what works and what doesn't."

I left his office. It was the middle of the day on a Tuesday. I'd switched back to seeing Dr. Summer twice a week. I called my office to let them know I was taking the day off, then went directly to the grocery store that I had tried on Saturday morning. There were far fewer cars in the parking lot, and I sat in my car and made up a grocery list. In the store I felt nervous but had no fuzziness or pain. I liked this grocery store because the aisles were wide. I tried hard not to look at everything, instead breaking my list down into categories. When I was in the produce aisle, I only looked at one side at a time and then refocused on the list to see if I needed anything from that section. Then I went to the other side, and anytime I started feeling the tightness in my chest, I focused on the list again.

Going up and down each aisle systematically this way made it easier for me. I could take my time. That felt very important, though I wasn't sure why. It was compelling not to feel rushed, to be in deliberate control. I knew by this time that strong, compelling feelings come from parts, so I took my time and made a mental note to talk to Dr. Summer about the issue.

About halfway through the store, I had a cartful of groceries. I would have everything on my list after a stop in the meat section. But I was tired. The store stacked things so high. The packaging was colorful but overstimulating. The tightness in my chest was building. I tried to focus on my list but a thought came: *I have to leave.* I had done as much as I could for that day.

I turned around and pushed my cart toward the cash registers. I unloaded my groceries, paid, and left. At home, I heard a small voice in my head say, "Thank you." I thanked the parts for letting me go to the grocery store. Even though we had left earlier than planned, I was elated to have accomplished something I hadn't been able to do in over a year. I had gotten everything on my grocery list except the meat.

In this way, I gradually exposed myself to greater and greater challenges. In the long term, negotiating with parts was a crucial strategy that helped me reenter activities I had given up. Things improved when I didn't fight with the parts, waging a kind of internal battle over panic attacks and the pain triggered by situations that seemed to match past traumas. I found that establishing their trust by demonstrating that I could and would listen to their fears and concerns, while still pushing my limitations, took us together toward a sense of being able to take care of ourselves and each other.

For a long time, I continued to struggle quite a bit with grocery shopping and large stores in general. When I couldn't reassure younger parts that they were safe, I bargained with them to help me do what I needed to do. *If you let me go to the electronics store and just buy this one item, I'll stop for ice cream on the way home.* Young parts could hold on for ice cream.

In our sessions, Dr. Summer and I focused on what parts felt, knew, and needed to share and on integrating and continuing to live my life to its fullest. He encouraged me to continue running and entering races, even though parts were afraid of crowds. He challenged me to continue my workouts at the gym.

Slowly, through continued efforts, I learned to challenge the fear inside and take positive steps to address it. I learned to set boundaries with people at work and at home. I learned to communicate with parts inside and orient them to what year it was and how safe I was now.

I also learned that blatantly ignoring the fear wasn't a helpful strategy—it pushed me too far too fast. When a friend of mine and I were in Indianapolis visiting his parents, I was proud of being able to make the trip out of town and stay with relative strangers. Greg and I both loved football, and his parents knew I was especially fond of the Colts. His mom managed to get Greg and me tickets to the game that weekend, with seats on the fifty yard line. I was touched by her gift, but inside I felt alarm and fear. The thoughts that came up from the parts were unmistakable: *We've never been there. We don't know what to expect. There will be lots of people. We want to stay here and watch the game. We already went along with the plan to come here to Indiana. We were told that if we came here, we could hang out with Greg's dad and watch TV all weekend. This is a change.*

I dismissed these thoughts. I wanted to go. These were amazing seats, and I didn't want to admit to either Greg's mom or myself that I needed to take some time to approach this more thoughtfully. So off we went.

As we drove to the stadium, though, my chest tightened and I felt slight pain at thoughts of how unsafe we would be. I noticed the feelings and reminded parts what year it was and who I was with. Greg knew about my childhood sexual abuse and my current-day panic attacks and was always thoughtful and helpful. He was tall and strong and safe. He would help protect us. I brushed away the fear parts felt about being around men who smelled of alcohol— parts that had experienced gang rapes by my brothers' friends or that had been prostituted. Because I wasn't closely listening to their fears, I didn't fully understand the experience of the parts that were actively trying to get my attention.

As we got closer yet, I felt more pain. I was stubborn and really wanted to go, and I didn't want to disappoint Greg or his parents. I continued to ignore the signs inside of me. We got our food and set off to find our seats. Looking around, I noticed that just about everyone was rowdy, drinking beer, and having a great time. I knew this was all fine and perfectly safe, but when we sat down the pain got worse. When we stood for the national anthem, I panicked. My thoughts raced, my head filled with cotton, and my eyes became unfocused. I wanted to jump out of my skin. Greg could see the panic and that I was in pain. He asked me what we should do. I barely managed to say, "Get me out of here!" The pain in my abdomen and back was unbearable.

Greg grabbed my hand and pulled me into the closest bathroom, making sure it was the ladies' room. Greg apologized to a woman washing her hands and explained that I was sick. She looked at me and said she understood. He opened a stall for me and firmly but kindly told me to sit in there and lock the door. He reassured me that he would wait right there. Inside the stall I felt a little better. Greg was so sweet. I could see his feet under the door of the stall and he stood there protecting me. Each time I heard the cheers of the crowd, pain surged through me and I couldn't stop shaking and crying. Greg asked if I was okay.

I said, "Not yet," and slowly took deep breaths.

I focused on the parts inside. They were mad that they'd had to do so much to get my attention. *We don't feel safe. Men smelled like alcohol. We can't trust you. You said you'd protect us. You didn't listen.* I felt bad. I had lost the trust of some of the parts.

"Okay, I understand," I said softly so Greg wouldn't hear. "It doesn't matter to you that I'm big and that Greg can help protect us, right?"

No one can protect us from all those people. We have to go.

"Do you know what year it is?"

We don't care.

"Okay, we'll leave." As soon as I said it, I stopped shaking, the pain eased, and I could breathe better.

Exhausted, I opened the stall door. Greg looked at me, worried. My heart went out to him. I'd scared him, and he was trying so hard to help.

"I am going to have to go. Is that okay?"

"Yes, of course. Is it the crowd?"

I started crying again. "I'm so sorry I couldn't do this, Greg."

"I don't care. I was happy watching it from home with Dad." We got home in time to watch the fourth quarter.

I learned over and over again to listen to parts. If I had taken the time to address their fear when it first came up, I might have been able to go to that game. I could have oriented them to what year it was before they started to feel panicky and let them know that they weren't being taken somewhere to be prostituted. I could have talked with Greg about the fears and maybe arranged for him to help me watch for unsafe conditions. This would have reassured younger parts that they were safe.

I would get much better at this, but there would still be times when pain from parts tried to get my attention. In those moments, I learned to be strategic about how much to resist, how much to nego-tiate, and how much to compromise, always trying to balance my bigger goals of building trust among my remaining parts and expand-ing my capacity to do things. I also continued to struggle with the idea of having any limitations at all. At times, when I found myself unable to do something that seemed effortless for others—some-thing that even I used to be able to do before I recovered all the memories—I felt utterly hopeless and without coping skills, losing sight of how incredibly far I'd come.

But I made a lot of progress. Even though crowds continued to be hard for me, I went to the state fair with hundreds of thousands of other people. I loved going and thought carefully beforehand through any fears that might come up—some that had come up with newly discovered parts and some that seemed predictable because I'd had panic attacks before. But I loved going to the fair. I ate pork chops on a stick, looked at all the chickens and llamas, and genuinely had a great time.

14

The first time I ever spoke publicly about my childhood experience was in 1996. I was still in therapy but beginning to function well again. I was stronger and had a much better sense of who I was and what had happened to me. I'd spent a lot of time trying to understand how my family could do what they did.

I got my start in public speaking when Veronica, my boss at the Office of Victims of Crime, stopped by my office to talk. We chatted for a few minutes before she asked, "So, how are you, really?"

"I'm doing well, thanks."

"Olga, when you first came to me with the offer of hiring you, I jumped at the chance because of what you were doing, because you wanted to heal. I hoped that you might get strong enough to share with others what you've learned about the violence you survived. Do you think you feel strong enough? Would you consider talking to service providers about child abuse from the perspective of a survivor?"

"Really?"

"Yes, I think you would be great."

I thought about it for a few minutes. "Yes, I think so."

"Do you think you could attend a meeting in St. Louis? It's about families in which there is both domestic violence and child abuse. Do you think you could go and talk about your experience?"

I thought about it again for a few minutes. "Yes, I think I can talk about it. I'm not sure about flying, though. That's a little scary."

"Let me know whether you think you'll be able to fly. Either way, I'd like you to oversee the grant projects that we have involving child abuse."

"Okay, I'd like that." I was excited to be working on these kinds of projects. Veronica seemed confident in my abilities. *Maybe I could make a difference.* Veronica smiled and left the room.

I sat there holding on to Veronica's words. *Will people really care what I think? Will they care what I have to say? I'm a lawyer, not a psychologist. This is an amazing opportunity. But do I want strangers to know about my DID? Maybe we can just talk about the abuse and not about the parts.* There was agreement inside that we would share about the abuse we suffered but not about the parts inside.

The next day, I sat in Dr. Summer's office waiting while he made tea. I was excited to tell him about my new assignment. As he handed me my cup, I started filling him in: "Veronica wants me to handle all the grants we have on child abuse. She thinks I have something to add to the projects that others in the office don't have." I paused to study his reaction. He carefully sipped his tea. When he was concerned about something I was doing, he usually got a more serious look on his face, where his eyes widened a little and the lines on his forehead showed up. It was a subtle look, but I could detect it. That day he didn't seem concerned.

"That sounds great, Olga. What's interesting to me is how surprised you seem. You do have a perspective that others don't have. You know this can happen, how it happens, and what helped you survive."

I sat there and thought about what he'd said. "She wants me to attend a meeting in St. Louis and make a speech. It's a great opportunity, and I think I want to do it."

"I'm sensing some hesitation. Are you worried about going?"

"Do you think people will listen to a lawyer talking about the impact of child abuse? Do you think they'll care what I think? I'm not you, Dr. Summer."

He smiled at my obvious statement. *Of course, I'm not him.*

"No, what I mean is, I'm not a psychologist. I don't have any training."

"That's not true," he interjected. "You have lots of training. You have survived years of abuse and have several years of therapy behind you. You know more than a lot of clinicians and researchers. You know what it feels like. You know what's helped you heal."

I was silent. "I'm scared, Dr. Summer."

"What are you scared of?"

"Everything. I'm afraid of feeling it all again. I'm afraid of saying it again."

"Do you think saying it will make it real?"

"Yes."

"Olga, it is real. As you live, grow, and continue to integrate, you'll increasingly feel how real this is and how it all did happen to you. The more you're able to feel in general, the more you'll feel good about things in your life," he reminded me. "At the same time, you'll also feel the bad in your life, and it will hurt more. That's the catch. You aren't dissociating as much anymore. So you may feel more upset if you do this. But I believe it will help your ability to feel things, including the good things. And you have the opportunity to help others."

I felt the familiar urge to avoid doing something new, something that might be unsafe in so many unpredictable ways. But I had been learning how to push through these feelings by listening carefully to parts and being creative about soothing their fears. When I was able to make it through a feared experience without panicking, the parts inside saw that it was okay and trusted me a bit more. Gradually I'd been able to do more and more new things.

"I'm worried about the plane." I paused and corrected myself: "Younger parts are scared to fly."

"What are they afraid of?"

"Planes are small and full of people. You have to sit in them and you're trapped. They're afraid of being trapped." I paused as I listened to other voices inside. Dr. Summer started to respond but I stopped him. "Other parts are afraid of getting sick on the plane. We got sick all the time when people hurt us, and Popi beat us when we got sick. So the idea makes me feel panicky."

"I can help you with that. The hypnosis and imagery we've used when you get really upset can help you stay calm and avoid panic. I can make a tape for you to listen to when you get on the plane. You can imagine that you're in a calm place while you're on the ground, taking off, and flying, and then wake up once you hear the announcement that you're in St. Louis. Would that make it easier for you to go?"

"Yes. That would be great."

"Okay. During our next session we'll make the tape."

"Thank you, Dr. Summer. But what if the tape doesn't work? What if my parts break through the hypnosis?"

"Then you can take a Klonopin to ease any anxiety parts might be feeling."

In 1996, I flew to St. Louis with the help of Dr. Summer's tape. I didn't panic, and I didn't need the Klonopin.

●　◦　●

In St. Louis, I spoke about watching my father beat my mother and then sexually abuse me. I chose not to talk about how my brothers abused me or, for that matter, anything that happened after my father died. I also didn't talk about being prostituted. That felt too complicated and raw, and I wasn't yet ready to talk about it to a big group of strangers and answer the inevitable questions. Listening to parts about what they're comfortable sharing, and thinking carefully about what I talk about when, is another way I demonstrate to parts that I'll help keep them safe and maintain their trust in me. That day, I simply told the audience what I could in general terms: "I was one of the children whom we will be talking about over the next couple of days. I watched in agony as my father did horrible things to my mother. And I endured the sexual attacks my father perpetrated on me. So as we move forward, I want to remind you why and for whom we are here."

I felt powerful being able to say just that. Looking back at it, I didn't give a lot of information about what happened. I didn't say much. But at the time it felt like a lot to me and I felt strong for doing it.

Only later did I find out that the audience included some of the foremost experts on domestic violence and child abuse. If I had known, I would have felt too vulnerable and wouldn't have agreed to speak. But throughout the ensuing meeting, the dialogue kept turning to me. As people discussed their ideas, someone would turn to me and ask, "Would that have helped you?" I'd think about the question and answer it to the best of my ability. It was an amazing feeling to be asked my opinion about such important issues, but it left me exhausted. The meeting lasted all day, and as folks went to dinner, I went up to my room instead. They had been talking about helping children and their mothers, and I had been talking to them about me. *This is my life. I don't get a break from it at dinner.* I sat in the dark in my room and cried so hard I was afraid someone in the hallway would hear me.

Back in Dr. Summer's office, he reminded me about the importance of experiencing that level of emotion and congratulated me on staying present and not dissociating through the entire trip. "It became more real to you."

"Yes, I could feel I was actually talking about me and not someone else."

"I know you probably can't feel this right now, but that was good. Olga, you are mourning the family you never had and the childhood you never had. I'm sorry for your pain."

I started crying. "When will it stop hurting?"

"I don't know. I wish I could tell you. I wish I could take the pain away. But it will get better and easier for you over time."

After that meeting, I received a number of requests from judges' groups, child welfare administrators, and domestic violence organizations to tell my story at their conferences. I agreed to most of them. Each time I felt stronger, appreciated for my insight, and increasingly sad for what my life had been like.

Even after Veronica left OVC, I continued to work on the projects we funded on domestic violence, sexual assault, and child abuse. I also helped obtain funding for programs whose goals were to assist women in immigrant and migrant worker communities, who are particularly vulnerable to coercion because of their immigration and economic status. My new boss allowed me to continue speaking out about my abuse. Each speaking engagement remained a very powerful experience for me. I got better at the way I presented and started showing snapshots of myself as a child so people could see and connect to the little girl inside of me. Over time, I was able to tell more about my experience and I think I became a better speaker, reading audiences and adjusting my speeches accordingly. I got used to the routine of airports and flying. After several months I didn't need Dr. Summer's tape anymore; I could hypnotize myself. I would get on the plane and put my briefcase away, then sit down, take a deep breath, and close my eyes. I would slowly fall asleep and usually sleep through the entire flight. It felt good.

After about seven years at OVC, I left the federal government to become an independent consultant and dedicate myself to working full-time on issues of child abuse, domestic violence, sexual assault, and trauma. Soon afterward, I finally had the courage to start talking about how I developed dissociation as a coping mechanism as a child and carried that through my life. I talked about being trained to initiate and accommodate abuse and about how these coping mechanisms carried over for me as a teenager and young adult. I showed audiences how dissociating put me at higher risk for attacks in my neighborhood and at school, making me more easily identified by sexual predators. I finally talked about my brothers and the gang rapes. I started adding a question-and-answer session to the end of my presentations, and I was touched by the thoughtful, caring questions people asked. I created a website describing the training, presentations, and technical assistance I offer.

For years I described dissociation but didn't talk about the disorder. Sometimes I could tell from people's questions that they knew I must have developed DID to survive, but they didn't ask outright. I didn't discuss it publicly until 2005, when I released the training video *A Survivor's Story* and submitted an article to the National Sexual Violence Resource Center newsletter about my life with DID. When I finally came out, I did it in a big way.

The response was greater than I expected. I received emails and requests to make presentations from all over the country. It felt good, and I no longer worried about being a lawyer talking about psychological issues, because I was talking from my experience, from the inside out. This has become my life's work.

Epilogue

I lie in my hotel room in Atlanta, missing home. *I hate being away.* I get up and focus on preparing for the day, running through the event in my head. It's a statewide conference for social workers with 250 participants. I will be presenting a keynote address about the impact of trauma from a personal perspective and leading several workshops on trauma and DID from an insider's point of view.

I love this work. As much as I hate to be away from home, I remind myself that I am in a unique position to help professionals understand how trauma and DID can appear, how they can recognize the signs of trauma, and how to work more effectively with people who have DID. For example, people who speak about a violent rape in a monotone with a flat demeanor are acting normally if they dissociated through the attack. Police officers and prosecutors can grow to understand that even when a person doesn't act the way they think a victim should, a crime still may have occurred.

My presentations have continued to expand in the last several years. I show pictures of myself as a child and end with a slideshow of my life now: facilitating workshops, standing at podiums telling my story, and spending time on the farm with Casey, the love of my life.

When I'm away, I miss Casey so much it hurts. She's an amazing partner—smart, witty, thoughtful, compassionate, and loving. Over the years, she has shown me how to be a better partner. When parts of me come forward, she isn't scared and points out changes in me. Thanks to our relationship, I'm getting even better at identifying parts.

We first worked together years ago—long-distance and without meeting in person. As I got to know her over the phone, I discovered her kindness and capacity for caring. I didn't realize it at the time, but I started to fall in love with this wonderful woman before we even met. I'll never forget seeing her for the first time. I was in Minnesota for a conference and had arrived a little later than I expected, so the training was just about to start. I was a bit flustered. Around me, people were checking in. Faculty members were going over the agenda, and others were taking care of last-minute details. It was so much to take in all at once. Then, in the midst of all the activity, Casey walked up and introduced herself. When I looked up to greet her, I was stunned. It was almost cliché, like in the movies when the whirl of activity around two characters stops. She exuded calmness in the midst of chaos.

I was reminded of Doña Graciela's eyes and her gentle soul full of kindness and love, unlike anything I had experienced before. I had found kindness in many people's eyes since then, but that day as I looked in Casey's eyes, I felt like I had been looking for her all my life. *I finally found her.* After my marriage ended some ten years before, it hadn't surprised me at all that I developed an interest in dating women. I was living alone for the first time in my life, and in that space, I realized I was attracted to women and had been since I was twelve years old. In my family and my culture, however, it never would have been okay to be a lesbian.

In Minnesota, I spent most of that conference talking to Casey as much as I could, while also trying not to appear too obvious. When I returned home, I realized that my life was missing something and soon afterward decided to move to Minnesota. For several years I had been wanting to leave the D.C. area, with its clogged highways and extravagant cost of living. The timing had just never been right. This was the perfect opportunity, and I had long been drawn to the Midwest, with its kind people and more relaxed approach to life.

I loved St. Paul and loved being close enough to Casey to see her occasionally. It took me a long time to tell her how I felt for fear of scaring her away and losing our connection altogether. Being her friend was better than not having her in my life at all. Finally, we shared with each other our mutual feelings and, soon after, bought a small farm that we renovated. In the last few years, we've established an organic berry patch and wonderful vegetable and herb gardens. We make soap, raise bees, and keep a small flock of chickens for eggs. Our small, farm-based business, Mirasol Farm, sells our organic soaps and lotions. We have three dogs and two cats. It's beautiful and peaceful and unlike any life I'd ever imagined for myself.

●　○　●

Shortly after I moved to Minnesota, my mom called. She said that she missed me. In 1994, in the depth of my therapy, I wrote my brothers and mother, describing the recovery process I was in and asking for their support. I explained the process as best I could, recommended a few therapists who could help them better understand DID, and gave them a list of books. I told them that without their support, I couldn't have a relationship with them. I never heard back from any of them.

When my mom called, now almost twelve years later, she didn't mention the letter or ask about my progress. Still, I was grateful to her for reaching out and felt hesitantly thrilled at the possibility of having a loving relationship with her on adult terms. For about six months, we were reunited. I visited her home and we spoke on the phone several times. Our conversations were very powerful for me. She said that she was sorry for all that happened when I was growing up, and I proudly filled her in on my career, my accomplishments, the work I was doing, and how it felt so meaningful. Before I knew it, I had bought her a new camera and set up a bank account for her in which I regularly deposited money. I did these things without thinking, without a plan. The urge to do them was compelling.

The last time we spoke, she left me a message on my forty-sixth birthday. I was so moved that she remembered my birthday that I cried harder than I had in years. When I returned her call, she told me her computer was broken and she couldn't afford to replace it. My heart fell. As I had done so many times before, I went to her rescue. Still on the phone, I went online and bought her a new laptop, top-of-the-line. That was what she had really called for. She thanked me and hung up. I went to Casey, sobbing. Soon afterward, I closed the bank account and asked my mom to not ask me for any more gifts or money. Now my relationship with my mom is very limited, and it's still very painful for me. She continues to occasionally send me bills she can't pay. I respond by telling her that I love her but I cannot pay her bills. My brother Mike handles her finances, and I suggest that she go to him.

●　◦　●

I haven't yet completely worked through the mechanism in me that mistrusts others, the one that came between David and me. Sometimes it's hard to trust Casey, to trust our friends, and even to trust Dr. Summer. I think I'll struggle with this my whole life.

I stopped working with Dr. Summer a couple of years before I moved to the Midwest. It had been a while since we'd found new parts and a long time since I had experienced the pain of panic, and I really thought that I was completely whole—that everyone inside me had been welcomed and integrated into who I was. But my first Christmas with Casey was hard and indicated otherwise. We spent the day with two families Casey had known for a long time, people who were becoming close friends of mine. I hadn't thought through what the day would be like. I'm not even sure what I expected. When we got there, the intimacy and chaos of eight adults and three children overwhelmed me. Something inside of me changed, awakening a part that looks for danger in unpredictable situations. I didn't notice the signs; my feelings seemed perfectly normal.

My thoughts morphed from being loving and caring to negative and angry. The delight I had taken in the kids and the appreciation I had for how much everyone had welcomed me into their lives were gone. These kind people seemed like a threat to me and my safety. I became inflexible. I felt almost as though I was sitting inside a shell, and if anyone made an unexpected sound or movement, the shell protecting me would break. I became quiet, internally disapproving, and impatient. The laughter and joy of gift giving annoyed me. Lingering together as the day went on made me impatient. I found myself getting angrier and angrier but didn't want to leave for fear of looking like a jerk and hurting everyone's feelings. Casey seemed to be in no rush to go. *It's her fault I'm stuck in the middle of this chaos. Casey knows me well enough now that she should have known this would be hard for me. She should have told me that it was going to be like this.* When we finally got home, I shared all my thoughts with Casey, and not in a kind way. I was angry at her for letting me down and leaving me miserable.

At that moment, Casey was two-dimensional to me. I felt hurt and withdrew, believing I was totally unimportant to her. Then I started to doubt who Casey was to me. I forgot that she was the love of my life, the woman who helped me build this life on a beautiful farm with all of our pets. I forgot that she was the one who generously shared her family and close friends with me. Swimming in uncertainty and suddenly very alone again in the world, my hard shell came up: *She cares about her friends more than she cares about me. I'm not a priority to her, just like I've never been a priority to anyone.* I had thought I was a priority to her and felt desperate to clear up this inconsistency. I had all sorts of questions. Casey tried to help clarify and explain, but she became hurt and guarded in response to my angry tone, unfeeling quality, suspicious questions, and talk of inconsistency.

It took a while, days really, but finally I could see that a mistrustful part had come up that I hadn't known about. Casey had seen the changes in me and tried to help me figure out what was happening. I realized I wasn't as completely integrated as I'd thought. I called Dr. Summer soon afterward, and we decided to continue working together over the phone.

I'm discovering that all of this new safety and stability—moving far away from where I had been hurt so badly, having a profoundly intimate relationship, finding a new community of people who welcome and love me—has allowed me to do even deeper work than I've done before. Being strong and in a safe place gives parts that I didn't know existed the chance to come forward with their memories. Ironically, their memories are the most painful to date. The mistrust these parts feel is very entrenched, and intended not to be detected by me. But the stronger I am, the more my mind knows I can handle the challenge.

Although I've made big improvements since that first Christmas, I struggle with habitual mistrust even today. Often Casey sees a change in me—something different in my facial expression, my tone of voice, the words I choose—before even I notice, and she gently asks me how I'm doing. Sometimes all I need is to be reminded of who she is. At other times, the reminder doesn't help and I'm unable to let the suspicions go. I ask questions over and over again until they're answered in a way that acknowledges the inconsistency. Now, however, I'm fully aware of my trust issues and Casey is too. Dr. Summer also knows them well. Sometimes I catch myself mired in negative, suspicious thoughts and can let Casey know that my trust issues are up. I can usually keep them under control when that happens. But when I can't anticipate them and can't keep them from coming up, we usually argue, and Casey is often unable to penetrate my protective shell. It's very painful for both of us. Eventually, however, my shell dissolves, either through lots of discussion and compromise, or simply through the passage of time, and we make it through the hard times.

• • •

Here in Atlanta, as I stand at the podium, hundreds of people have chosen to be here on a Saturday—women and men of all ages, races, and professions, and I am moved. They work with children, the elderly, families in poverty, adults with developmental disabilities, and victims of violence. They work in schools, hospitals, public agencies, and nonprofit organizations. They are here to learn how to do their jobs better.

Suddenly I feel more nervous than I have all week. This is a very diverse audience. How can I take my experience and apply it to what they do? If I open their hearts, what message can I give them that would help? I'm not sure. But I have to get started. At an earlier time in my life, I would have automatically dissociated at this point. Instead, I feel the nervousness, stay present, and somehow, as if by magic or divine intervention, it almost always works out well.

"Thank you for having me here today. It is an honor to be among so many people who care so much that they are dedicating their weekend to this conference. I am here as a survivor to tell you about my experience of growing up in a home where my father perpetrated domestic violence against my mother and sexually abused me. I'm here as a person who coped in a way that allowed me to be here today but made me vulnerable to abuse when I was a teenager and young adult…"

Over the next hour, I tell them about my experience of abuse and survival. I describe Doña Graciela, her hugs, her love. I remind them that they can be the person who makes a difference in the lives of the children and adults they work with, often through simple, everyday acts involving praise, small gestures of affection, simple respect, and meaningful connections. Afterward, they tell me that they appreciate the message. I talk with them all day, formally in workshops and informally in hallways, at lunch, and even in the bathroom. I am honored by their stories and their dedication to alleviating suffering.

After the conference ends, one of the social workers takes me back me to the airport. I go through security and to my gate, where I wait patiently for my plane to load and take off. I still use the hypnosis that Dr. Summer taught me, so I sleep most of the way home. As I walk out of the airport, I see Casey waiting. My heart fills with love. I've missed her so much. I wave and get in the car grinning. In the backseat, our dog Griffin wiggles, licks my face, and croons at me in his special way. I lean over and kiss Casey, then relax in my seat as she drives us home. This is what I have always wanted: to be loved and love well in return. I have looked for this all my life, and I have finally found it. I am home.

Olga R. Trujillo is an attorney who works with communities on issues involving domestic violence, child abuse, sexual assault, and the impact of trauma. A nationally renowned speaker, she has appeared in several training videos on domestic violence, including *Cut It Out* and *A Survivor's Story*. She has received the Bud Cramer Leadership Award from the National Children's Alliance and the Sunshine Lady Foundation Peace Award. Olga lives with her partner Casey, dogs, and cats on a small farm in Wisconsin.